Becoming You

An Owner's Manual for Creating Personal Happiness

Dr. B. Marshall

iUniverse, Inc.
New York   Bloomington

Becoming You
An Owner's Manual for Creating Personal Happiness

Illustrations by A. Gustavson.

iUniverse books may be ordered through booksellers or by contacting:

iUniverse
1663 Liberty Drive
Bloomington, IN 47403
www.iuniverse.com
1-800-Authors (1-800-288-4677)

Because of the dynamic nature of the Internet, any Web addresses or links contained in this book may have changed since publication and may no longer be valid.

ISBN: 978-0-595-52632-1 (pbk)
ISBN: 978-0-595-51394-9 (cloth)
ISBN: 978-0-595-62684-7 (ebk)

Printed in the United States of America

iUniverse rev. date: 4/28/2009

CONTENTS

PREFACE

I began writing this book to help my students and clients take the small steps necessary to open their minds to the possibility of attaining lost dreams through everyday tasks. My own life has been such a wonderful journey of discovery, rediscovery, and goal attainment that I was stymied by the confusion, depression, and anger of those around me who could not see the road that was rising before them, waiting to be traveled.

My own story, touched by great joy as well as sorrow and loss, has been my foundation of hope. I lost both my parents when I was in my twenties, with my mother dying in my arms. I have lived through a failed marriage, multiple miscarriages, and raising a child with significant disabilities, and I'm now facing the age-related reality that I will not always be young and beautiful. In all of these challenging situations, I have been able to see the glass not as half full or half empty, but as a vessel that *I* need to fill. In each case of loss or disappointment, I stepped back and asked myself, "What do I want to have happen next? Who do I want to be in five years?"

The deaths of my parents six weeks apart, along with my failed first marriage, led me to travel the world for four years, experiencing new lands, new languages, new customs, and a rebirth of hope. When I returned to the United States, I went back to school for my first master's degree and met my best friend and life partner. The birth of our first child was a magical moment that I thought could happen only once in a lifetime, until our second child was born and that sense of awe and boundless love was reawakened. I had, like the phoenix, risen from the ashes and taken flight again.

When my oldest child was about eighteen months old, it became apparent that there was something not quite right with her development. When she fell on the playground, it took her a while to steady herself and get up, and sometimes she would just stare off into space. A nurse by profession, I began to document what I saw. No one, however, believed the new over-reactive mom, and I soon stopped believing myself. When she was two and a half, she experienced a partial complex seizure that lasted well over an hour. My husband and I rushed her to the hospital where, after IV medications, she finally was able to emerge from the seizure.

There is nothing more devastating then seeing your child helplessly thrashing, struggling for breath, and not being able to do anything. That was over fifteen years ago. She has since had hundreds of seizures and even stopped breathing once. On that day, when I had to perform CPR on my child, I understood that being happy *today* really matters. I considered of all the things that were beyond my control, but I thought that if I could give my children love and hope, then they would be able to create their own personal happiness. More than anything, I wanted them to have happy lives.

I enrolled in Teacher's College, Columbia University, to learn the skills that would enable me to help my children navigate this world. I wanted to get tools so that our family, would have the chance to have a good, *normal*, happy life, despite our critical barriers. I knew it was going to be a bumpy road, so I went back to school to reinforce the shocks and brakes on the vehicle that would takes us where we wanted to go.

The ten-year journey of getting my doctorate from Columbia was a powerful experience. The most valuable training that I received was from Dr. Dennis Mithaug, who taught me how to develop theories and explore methods to increase self-determined behaviors. As I listened to his lectures and worked with him on my dissertation, the sense of my future direction became clearer. Self-directed behavior demands planning, but consistent goal achievement rewards itself.

After I earned my doctorate, I began teaching behavior change at college. Year after year, hundreds of student passed through my course asking me to write a book. They wanted me to commit my theories and methods to paper so they could pass along the information to their families and friends. "After all, change cannot occur in a vacuum" they would chide.

I studied with Martin Seligman in his Authentic Happiness Coaching program and began coaching families and individuals in my private practice. Again my clients would scold me. "Dr. Marshall, you need to put this into a book!"

Yet there was something still missing. The power that nursing gave me to save my child's life was calling to me with a new voice. Coaching and psycho-education were helping my clients and students construct happy lives, but I wanted more—I wanted to be able to provide therapy for those who needed to expel their nightmares before they could enjoy their dreams. Recently, I have evolved into a psychiatric nurse practitioner, my final and highest degree. Now, as I navigate my future, I do so with the knowledge that I can provide guidance, therapy, or education. I can work with other families who are learning that the road they will travel with their exceptional children will be a happy one, filled with challenges but also filled with joy. There are detours we all need to take, but I can assure you, it's not how quickly you get to your destination, but that you choose the destinations with care and enjoy the ride.

When my daughter was asked whether she would be willing to repeat a grade to get into the high school of her choice, she replied that she would be okay with that. "You know," she said, "my mom is pretty old and *she's* still going to school. In our house we just keep learning until we get it!" Amen.

This book is dedicated to my students and clients who never stopped nagging me to write it; to my editors who kept me rewriting it; to my friends who keep asking me if they can come on Oprah and Ellen with me; to Alis, my piano teacher, who promised me that forty-something was a great age to learn piano; to my parents who taught me that the best gift a parent can give his or her child is a sense of accomplishment and independence; to my sisters who have consistently given me support and love on my voyage to becoming me; to my husband who keeps loving me and challenging me and supporting me in all my changes; and to my children—without whom I would never have learned how to grow and change to meet their needs, which in turn meets all of mine. Thank you, all.

CHAPTER 1

WOULD'VE, COULD'VE, SHOULD'VE, OR AM?

THE "BECOMING YOU" CHALLENGE

The key to happiness is learning how to bend with the wind and enjoy the experience as it's happening. It's about learning how to anticipate change, become accustomed to change, and finally embrace change as a welcomed life partner. There is great energy in change—sometimes so much energy that it can fill people with fear and dread and paralyze them in their tracks. But there's a better way to handle change. You can learn skills that will allow you to tap into the energy of change so that it can elevate, energize, and release you to become who you always wanted to be.

This book will help you love the thrill of change. It will enable you to feel the excitement of anticipation and to rise to the challenge of making what you want to have happen next actually come to be. Imagine going to sleep with the satisfied feeling that you are exactly who you wanted to be at this juncture of your life! Think about hitting that pillow with a smile on your face, content in the knowledge that you are moving toward becoming who you always wanted to be.

HOW TO EMBRACE CHANGE AS A LIFELONG PARTNER

Learning how to love change is a skill. Being able to define your goals and work toward them reflects your personal commitment to growth and self-determination. Even with a goal of becoming partners with change, it's important to have a stable set of values with healthy relationships as your anchors. This stability will allow you to lead a life that is enjoyable and fulfilling, while calmly adjusting to the changing currents of each day. You will start to take the time to think about what you want to have happen next in your life, and then you will plan the new courses to get there.

It's easy to spot a healthy, mindful, change-partner. Just look for the person who lets go of grudges, listens to what is being said, evaluates the situation for what is needed, and moves in a direction that will result in positive personal growth. Change-partners find their satisfaction in the creation of personal happiness. They recognize the need for personal evolution. They have skills that include letting go of false securities, developing self-determined behaviors, negotiating toward resolutions, and accepting compromise.

Now it's your turn. Are you living the life you always wanted? Are you who you want to be? Are you ready to take the challenge to turn your life around and begin to move in the direction that will bring you satisfaction and contentment?

This book is about honesty—your ability to see yourself, your motivations, your behaviors, your undermining alibis, and your crucial cover-ups for what they are: pathways to success or convenient excuses for failure. So the question still stands: have you become who you always wanted to be? Are you happy with your life today, or has the reality of who you have become fallen short of the person you once dreamed of being?

George Eliot once wrote, "It is never too late to become what you might have been." She understood that becoming who she wanted to be entailed sacrifices and hard work, and she also valued her goal enough to make the changes necessary to reach her dream. For many of us, this level of self-determined behavior has been elusive. The risks involved seem to outweigh the possibility of success, and so many of us take the more secure, seemingly easier road. The result of this choice often leaves us with a sense of dissatisfaction.

It's not unusual to hear parents telling their children, "You can become anything you want when you grow up". They tell their children to dream, when quite often they themselves are in the process of giving up, or have already given up, their own dreams.

A thirty-year-old woman begins to panic that she will never get married, so she says yes to a suitor she feels no real affection for. She forgets that the goal of marriage is to share a happy life with a loving partner, and because of her choices, she finds herself trapped in an unfulfilling relationship. Or look at the fifty-year-old man who has spent twenty years of his life working at a job that was only meant to support him while he finished his novel. He got detoured, got married, needed an income, forgot about the novel, and just settled into a tepid, stagnant pool of melancholy and discontent. Or look at the person who, at sixty-something, is facing loads of free time and no partner to share it with. Each of these stories reflects outcomes of dreams denied, deferred, or dashed.

Over the years, I have listened repeatedly to stories of dashed hopes. Students, clients, and patients have come to speak with me about their passions, hopes, dreams, and disappointments. I hear the anger and self-pity that comes from years of unfulfilled yearning for goals never achieved. I see the depression and the chronic feelings of worthlessness, self-hatred, and despair that come from thinking success is no longer possible. But I'm here to tell you that solutions, resolutions, and answers do exist. In fact, you can often find the answer in changes that start small but become the steady first steps along the road to hope. You start by navigating that initial, small, acceptable first step. When that step feels comfortable, you identify and take on a second one, and then a third. At first, you might feel uncomfortable with that sense of achievement and self-worth, and your boring old life, with all its problems and sadness, may sometimes call to you. However, your ability to create your own happiness will guide you toward positive, self-determined behavior and the need for change.

Throughout this book, I will recount many stories of change. Some may sound surprisingly familiar, and you might think, "How did she know about me? That's *my* story." I hope you will see that each of us, to some degree, exists in every story.

STARTING ON THE ROAD TO BECOMING YOU

Let's start with you. Look at your life. What works in it? What makes you happy? Choose one aspect of your life, right now, that makes you happy.

For some, this task might appear difficult, but I ask you to think about one thing you do that fills you with a feeling of well-being—something that, when you're engaged in doing it, time falls away. Mihály Csíkszentmihályi describes this feeling as flow, when action and awareness are so seamless that time no longer intrudes on your thoughts.[1] This state of flow can occur whenever you are engaged in an action that brings you peace, such as reading a good book, talking to someone you love, or listening to music. Don't think about what you have to do in your day; think about what you love to do when you don't have to think about what you have to do. Now state out loud: I am happy when I _____. You might have to say it a few times before it feels comfortable.

OBSTACLES TO HAPPINESS

What gets in the way of being happy? Many excuses come to mind, but let's look at them one by one. During the course of this book, we will uncover the barriers you have constructed that are keeping you from achieving your fullest potential. Many of your barriers are hidden in habitual excuses, which you will have to uncover and dismiss. To help you do this, as we expose the excuse, you will be introduced to "Marshall's Laws." These guidelines can help you achieve happiness while you move toward becoming who you want to be. To become a partner of positive change, you will have to unlearn some your old coping skills that have become a wall between you and your happiness.

Why do we create barriers to happiness? It is not as if we do it consciously. It's easier to repeat past behaviors, even those that do not get us exactly to our goals, than to plan and engage in new behaviors. Each time we provide an excuse for why a goal wasn't achieved, we add another brick to the barrier. When our excuses are questioned, we sometimes tell a little white lie to help us from losing face. These tactics serve only to move us away from our goal. Rather than admitting when we have made mistakes, we repeat our excuses, which in turn fortifies the barrier. When we get used to having the barrier, we often lose sight of what our goal was to begin with. Furthermore, we align our thoughts and behaviors to be more in line with the excuse and the barrier than our goal.

I like to think of excuses and lies as the scaffolding that supports the obstacles that prevent us from achieving our goals. To remove the barriers between you and your happiness, you will have to find the courage and energy to dismantle the scaffolding.

Happy and/or Successful

Liam was a successful businessman. He had a wife, kids, and a house in the suburbs. His Labrador retriever, Bingo, barked and panted upon Liam's return each day. Life was good.

Liam came to my class at the encouragement of his wife, Janet. Janet explained that she had noticed that for some unknown reason, despite his denials, Liam seemed completely unsatisfied with his life. He would come home with very little energy, hardly talking to the family and never wanting to play with the kids.

I asked Liam what made him happy. "Everything," he answered. "My life is good ... really." But his facial expression lacked the enthusiasm I usually saw in truly happy people.

"Tell me," I pursued, "is there ever a time when you're engaged in doing something, and you lose track of time? You know, like it's ten in the morning and the next thing you know it's four in the afternoon?"

His eyes glazed over. "Well," he drawled, "I used to love to play the piano. I don't dare do it anymore, just because it made me lose control of time." The spark left his eyes, and he lowered his gaze.

His wife's shoulders slumped. "Time," she said. "There's never enough."

TIME

If I had a quarter for every instance "time" was blamed for keeping someone from achieving his or her goal or even a little piece of happiness, I'd be a millionaire a thousand times over!

> MARSHALL'S LAW #1: Lack of time is not a valid excuse.

The moment has come to stop using lack of time as an excuse! It's killing your ability to persevere toward a happy ending. You are working every day to convince yourself of what you *can't* achieve. What's worse is that by using lack of time as an excuse, and by repeating it to yourself and to everyone who will listen and gravely nod in agreement, you are creating the foundation for an *undermining alibi*.

THE UNDERMINING ALIBI

What is your happy ending? How do your lies interfere with you achieving it? Each of us develops behaviors to protect ourselves from perceived threats. For example, a child who knows that telling her parents she got a bad grade could get her punished, might present the situation as involving a cruel teacher who constantly picks on her. This tactic buys the child time to either study and correct the matter or simply blame the teacher.

In this example, those who correct themselves drop the "alibi" of the bad teacher and empower themselves to move toward success. However, there are some people who will find that this alibi gets them out of the work they need to do. They will persist in employing it throughout school, always blaming the teacher or the school and never accepting accountability for the work (or lack of it). When this happens, the alibi turns into what I call an "undermining alibi" because it ceases to protect you and actually undermines your ability to find success. The difference between a normal excuse (alibi) and an undermining alibi is that a normal excuse should only remove you from the high-risk situation and give you time to correct the problem. An undermining alibi, however, becomes a chronic lament. Over time it is the alibi that is empowered, not the individual. Through that transfer of power, the capacity to believe in yourself, to move to self-determined behavior, is lost.

As you read on, remember that the more you repeat your undermining alibis, the stronger they become. *To change the way things are and the way they will be, you need to let go of your undermining alibis. They are not protecting you; they are imprisoning you.*

So many of us frame what we want by stating what we don't want. For example, a person who wants to get in shape often states his goal as "I don't want to be fat and out of shape!" What if I tell you that by framing what you want in the negative, you are directing yourself away from your goal and oftentimes reinforcing your undermining alibis? It's the old "don't look at my nose" trick. You don't believe me, do you?

Okay, stop reading for a second and look at a person in the room, but *don't look at his or her nose.* Go ahead, just try.

See how much energy you have to expend to not look at the person's nose? Once you have the thought of what not to do, it's all that you *can* do! You plant the intrusive directive that undermines the focus of what you want to have happen next. That's why when teachers tell students not to watch the clock, they are in effect mandating the intrusive thought of "watch the clock, watch the clock, watch the clock." The guy who always states on the first date "I don't want to get married" will be constantly thinking about marriage, and so forth. So for those of us who prefer to see the positive potentials of each situation, we are usually able to manipulate or manufacture positive outcomes.

I say "usually" because it's not always possible. Life is not consistent or predictable, which is why your goal, and the path to achieve it, must be clearly stated in simple and direct terms.

To become what you want to be, you have to remember your true dreams and desires. At the end of the day, just before you drift off to sleep, what last thought involving the achievement of a personal goal would bring a smile to your face

Following are a number of behavioral goals to choose from, or you can write in your own. It's important that this goal be measurable, that it is concrete, and that it has a time frame. Someone should be able to see you meeting this goal, so "thinking" about something or someone would not belong on this list.

Goal

Lose one pound a week.
Call or e-mail family members each week.
Drink eight glasses of water a day.
End a bad relationship this month.
Pamper myself once a week with a massage.
Quit smoking over the next three months.
Save five dollars a week.
Get in shape by exercising thirty minutes a day.

The list is endless. Now concentrate on the present. Think about one thing you could do today that would give you a satisfied feeling of achievement if you accomplished it by the end of the day. Add it to the list and finish this statement:

At the end of the day, if I _____, I would be happy with myself.

Put this statement on your refrigerator, in your wallet, and anywhere that will cue you to engage in that behavior.

SUMMARY

When you find yourself feeling unsatisfied with your life, it is time to take back control over where you want it to go. By identifying what makes you happy and opening yourself up to the positive energy of change, you are able to start on the journey back to becoming who you always knew you were meant to be. To get to your goals, you will need to stop using lack of time as an excuse and start identifying one behavior that you can engage in, every day, that will remind you how it feels to be satisfied and happy with yourself.

CHAPTER 2

GOALS, ACTIONS, AND CHOICES

Goals

Barbara always wanted to be a dancer. At thirty-two, she found herself gainfully employed, in a somewhat satisfying relationship, and restless. Her partner did not enjoy dancing of any kind, so over their four-year relationship, Barbara danced less and less. As a child she remembered taking ballet classes, but she could not recall how old she was when the lessons stopped.

"I know I'm too old to become a dancer," she confided in me one day, "but I still have fantasies about it." Barbara and I set about making her "fantasy" of dancing a reality.

ONE GOAL, ONE BEHAVIOR

Some goals in life change because we change, while others seem elusive or are postponed because they are dependent on others for realization. When you consider establishing your goal, only consider goals that you can reach on your own. Because everything in life is so interdependent, it may be hard to imagine reaching a goal without help, but think about things you want to achieve for yourself. Some examples of a personal goal might be to lose weight, gain weight, get better grades, make more money, or have more leisure time. Once you are clear about the general idea of your goal, you can start to identify some specific steps towards achieving it. Of course, the first (and for some, the biggest) step is to clearly identify your goal.

IDENTIFYING YOUR GOAL

Verbalizing your goal is a good beginning. It's very important to state what you want, not what you don't want. The more simply you can state the goal, the better. Although Barbara didn't want to give up her job and become a professional dancer, she *did* want to reconnect with dancing as a source of personal joy.

To become who you've always wanted to be, you will need to remember what is was, or what it is, that *you* truly want. It's not about pleasing anyone else. When you look at your life, what was the dream that got deferred, as you became a responsible adult? Once you have identified one dream (many of us have multiple dreams, but let's start with just one), consider how you could incorporate that dream into your life right now. Do not use time as an excuse. Identify one goal you had for yourself that you gave up on. Then identify one behavior you could fit into your life today that would help you move toward that goal. Here are some examples:

GOAL	BEHAVIOR
To be a dancer	Take a dance class.
To live in France	Take a French course.
To be a pitcher for the Yankees	Join a softball team.
To write a best-selling novel	Write in a journal each day.

Before you continue reading, identify something you once wanted to be or do. This will be your goal. It needs to be independent of others and one that you are willing to work for. It cannot be a means to an end, but an end in and of itself.

IDENTIFYING A BEHAVIOR

When you have clearly identified that goal, finish this sentence: one behavior I can engage in today that will move me toward my goal is ____

_____

_____.

The behavior you've identified will be your **home-base behavior.** Engage in your home-base behavior at least once a day. Learning the skills that will help you become who you always wanted to be requires working on your home-base behavior. This beginning action reflects your commitment to yourself and provides you with a daily reminder of your direction. It also gives you the baseline against which you can later evaluate your progress.

Getting control of your behavior begins by increasing your awareness of when you act with the knowledge that you make your choices free from the dictates of others. This is called acting with self-determination. To experience the power of self-determined behavior, you will need to pace your changes. It is important to start with only one change; if you change many things at the same time, you lose your capacity to evaluate the effect of each change. Changing many things at the same time is a setup for failure. One change will be enough of a challenge for now.

Here is some important information regarding your behavior.

Behaviors Are Actions. A behavior is concrete, observable, and measurable. *Thinking* about dieting is not a behavior; it's a thought. *Wanting* another person to love you is not a behavior; it's a desire. A good rule of thumb about identifying a behavior is that if you can't see it and can't measure it, it's not a behavior.

- **One Behavior Only.** Only identify one behavior, not a chain of events.
- **Independent Behaviors.** Behaviors that rely on others build into them the failure excuse! Make sure your home-base behavior is something you can do, independent of others.

MARSHALL'S LAW #2: Your behavior cannot depend on someone else. You are in control of yourself, your choices, and your behavior. **Using other people as an excuse for not succeeding is no longer valid (and will, over time, turn into an undermining alibi).**

CHOICES

Your life is a reflection of the choices you have made. Like it or not, you have invented your life through the decisions and choices you have made and continue to make every day, every minute, and every second. In the next second, you will make a choice and begin to reinvent your life as you want it to be.

Finish the statements that follow:

My long-range goal, if all things in this world were possible, would be ___

_____.

My short-term goal, which I would like to accomplish in the next three months, is _____
_____.

The home-base behavior I can begin to engage in today, and for which I will do each day for the next three weeks, is _____
_____.

This behavior will help me move in the direction of my goal by _____
_____.

SUMMARY

Becoming who you want to be requires a clear idea of who that person is. Take the time to figure it out, and be clear about it. The more specific you can be, the easier it will be for you to start the journey to achieve it. This means that you will need to identify an independent goal and one first step to start you in the direction of achieving that goal. You need to repeat your home-base behavior each day until you are comfortable with it, aware of it, and committed to it. The behavior must be one that you can do independently of others and which brings you happiness at the end of the day. Your journey has begun; you've taken the first step.

CHAPTER 3

CHOICE OR CHANCE?

Teaching behavior change has allowed me to help hundreds of students become aware of the importance of choosing their destiny. I often had students share with me how their lives were changing during the course, reinspiring me to keep my choices alive. Becoming who you want to be is not a passive activity! Self- awareness can be the spark that reminds you to question where your life is going. It is easy to fall into repeating old patterns, but if you keep alert you will know when you are actively choosing your path and when you are blaming your situation on "chance."

Lost and Found

"I feel totally lost," Zach said with a sigh as he leaned on my office door. "I'm glad you're still here." Our class had just ended, and he looked very sad, so I invited him to sit down and asked him to explain what he meant.

"Well, I came to New York because of the death of my father. He was a mean bastard, and he was quite ill with cancer for a long time. My mother needed me to stay close to home and help her care for him." His eyes welled up with tears. "I hated him. I hated my life. I spent my life waiting for him to be gone so I could escape. As soon as he died, I left Oklahoma and decided to just keep moving east. When I got to New York City, I felt like I could just get lost in the crowd. I moved in with an old friend. She goes to school here, and she convinced me to take some courses, too. I haphazardly signed up for yours. Today when I was in your class, though, I realized how many dreams I gave up because of my parents and their demands on me. Now I'm in the same rut at my friend's house, and *she* is making demands on me! Dr. Marshall, I feel like a failure—a homeless, weak failure. I don't want to go back to Oklahoma, but I'm just as miserable here! I feel like I will never be able to be happy!"

His shoulders crumpled. "Please help me. I need to get a life, Dr. Marshall. I want to be happy."

CHOOSING CHANGE

Sometimes, when people feel as though they have lost everything, they find the courage to change. But *I* know that it's easier to change before all hope is gone (though many of us lack that motivation prior to feeling totally hopeless) and a heck of a lot less expensive. The secret is that we have to *choose* to change and then consistently choose to stay on course.

The goal of this chapter is to help you discover your strengths in decision-making, so that you will successfully choose the behaviors that will help you reach your goals. You have been making decisions all your life, so my question to you is this: why did some turn out great and others awful?

One of my clients who was in her forties told me that when she was sixteen she had no idea that she would spend the next two decades of her life dating. Before she met her husband, she became involved in relationship after relationship, and each ended in heartache. Every time she met a guy she would go down a list of must-haves and would-be-nice-ifs. *If* he passed the test, she would date him. Invariably, by the sixth month of dating, her must-haves became should-haves and either she or the man lost interest. Finally, after twenty years, she found her match. And guess what? He had been there most of the time! He was the friend who picked her up after each failed relationship. He won her over by opening her eyes to her choices and then by becoming the best choice for her.

REVIEWING PAST CHOICES

Now back to you. It's time for you to review some of your life's choices. First, look at the decisions you have made that worked for you. What do they have in common? Now look at some of the disasters. What do they have in common?

People don't often take the time to actually think about what goes on each time they make a decision. This lack of awareness about the decision-making process is often the culprit for people repeatedly making poor choices. Continuing to automatically repeat the same behavior over and over makes the anticipation of a new outcome pretty ridiculous—but most of us still do it anyway!

The following diagram indicates the process that *should* take place for you to make decisions that lead to a desired outcome. First, you identify your immediate goal, and then you take into consideration your present situation and your intention, or what you are preparing to do. It is important for your intention to reflect your desire to get to your goal, not respond to your present situation! Once you are clear on that, you identify at least three choices and then decide upon the one that will move you toward your goal. All too often our intention gets hijacked toward responding to the present situation, and that rarely helps us get to our intended goal.

Imagine a quarterback is about to throw the football to his receiver when one of the defensive linebackers calls the quarterback's mother a name. The quarterback can respond to the linebacker, which would change all the choices and actions, or he can focus on passing to his teammate and getting to his original goal. The choice is his, but the outcome related to his action will affect the whole team, regardless of which choice he makes.

Like the quarterback, you always have multiple choices in any given situation and the final choice is yours to make. If you choose not to make a decision, that is a decision as well. The outcome that you and those around you experience will be related to the final decision, which will reflect either your commitment to the goal or your impulse to react to the present situation. It's all a matter of self-awareness. The more aware you are of your goal, and the more committed you are to acting in ways that will move you to it, the better you will get at making self-determined choices.

THE DECISION-MAKING GRID

The following grid is helpful to use as you're becoming aware of the kind of decisions you are making. It allows you to map out your decisions and assign power to your intentions. I suggest that you use both the map and the written narrative in the beginning. After a few decisions, your mindfulness, or awareness of how your intention drives your choice, will become apparent. The following grid will outline the decision-making of the quarterback.

The areas of importance are: Determining your goal, Identifying the present situation: Clarifying your intention: Identifying at least three possible choices that you have, as well as their likely outcomes and then choosing the action that moves you towards your goal. Your honesty is crucial for this decision grid to help you move in the right direction, taking responsibility for the consequences of your decisions.

THE DECISION GRID

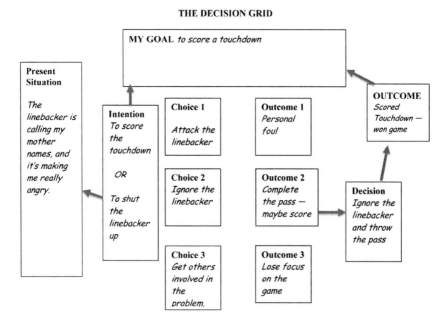

Narrative:

My goal: to pass the winning touchdown and win the game

The present situation: Emotions are running high. There's a guy on the other team calling my mother names, and it's making me really angry.

My intention: I have to decide whether I want to stay focused on the task at hand and score the touchdown, or call this guy out and settle the situation, reacting to him because I'm so angry.

- *Choice 1* Attack the linebacker.
  Likely outcome of choice 1 Personal foul—team penalty

- *Choice 2* Ignore him.
  Likely outcome of choice 2 Complete throw/score touchdown

- *Choice 3* Get others involved
  Likely outcome of choice 3 Everyone gets distracted, possible personal fouls, possible penalties, escalation of negative energy and emotions.

My decision: Ignore him and focus on completing the pass.

Actual outcome: TOUCHDOWN!

Know what you want to have happen next. Focus on your goal and stay aware of the kind of decision-making you're getting into. Many times our emotional self wants to react to a situation, while our more mature, adult self is weighing the options. Sometimes we are just repeating behaviors we learned as kids, without thinking what we want to have happen next. When you find yourself with a racing heart, sweaty palms, or short breaths, chances are you're on your way toward reacting impulsively. If you feel like you're zoning out, you probably won't act at all. In either case, get in touch with how your body is responding before you do anything. Once you take an action, it's hard to undo.

What Do You Want to Have Happen Next?

Dee and Jay were experiencing an ongoing problem with their relationship. Each day when Dee would come home, Jay would ask what was for dinner. Dee would look through the refrigerator and call out what was left over. Jay never liked the choices, so Dee would tell him, "Why don't *you* cook something if you don't like what I have?"

Exasperated, Jay would storm out of the house and buy food for Dee and himself at a nearby takeout. Dee has started coming home later from work, and Jay's been ordering in at least four times a week. Today's arguments were about Jay's weight, their lack of money, and how all their conversations are strained.

"How long has this been going on?" I asked

"Since we got married four years ago."

"Is it working for you? Are you happy?" I asked.

They both looked at the floor and whispered, "No."

"Tell me, how did it start?" I asked.

Dee looked at me and said, "When I was a kid, my mother had to cook every night, as well as work, and I wasn't going to fall into that trap. Finally when my mother stopped cooking, my father got the message and stopped expecting dinner on the table. I wanted to make sure we didn't have the same expectations in our marriage."

Jay's eyes widened. "Your parents are divorced, though. Is that what you wanted for us?"

Dee began to cry. "No, I guess I just did what I knew how to. I didn't think about the end of their marriage, just about how to stop the fighting when I was part of it."

"Did you think repeating this scene day after day would suddenly deliver a different outcome?"

Dee looked at me. "I don't know … I just fell into the habit, I guess. I didn't really think about what was going to happen."

Jay nodded in agreement. "The whole thing was like a roller coaster ride. Day after day, we bought our tickets and let it take us away. What can we do to stop it? We really do love each other." He looked at Dee. "I don't want to live like this anymore." She nodded in agreement.

"Okay, tell me other scenes that can happen when you get home from work, but before saying anything, ask yourself, What do I want to have happen next?"

Within minutes we were on our way toward creating alternative choices that would lead to the life Dee and Jay had dreamed of having with each other.

It is astounding how many people repeat unsuccessful choices and wonder why they have not yet achieved their goal. If you don't know what you want to have happen next, it is hard to plan the course to get there. It's like getting in your car without knowing what your destination will be. You just sit there, if you start the car and drive, you don't know where you will end up. If this is your style, hopefully you think enough in advance to get the gas tank filled.

SUMMARY

Choosing your future is not a passive activity. You need to be aware of your past and actively engaged in the present to direct yourself toward the future of your choice. Falling into old habitual behaviors and familiar situations will provide you with the comfortable feeling of "sameness," but it will not help you change the path of your future. It will get you stuck in a rut that fuels discontent. Before making a choice, identify at least three possible alternatives and visualize where each one will take you. When you decide which path to take, remember that you can change your mind and your actions if the course begins to resemble the road to your past.

CHAPTER 4

SNAP, HABIT, OR PLANNED?

No matter what you intend to do, each action you take is based upon a decision. Some of the decisions we make are deliberate, but many are instinctive or don't involve much preplanning. Even the lack of deciding is in actuality a decision that has real consequences.

Life is all about decision-making. Everything that happens to you in your life can be traced back to the decisions you have made or chosen not to make.

I have identified three distinct styles of decision-making. All choices fall into one of these three categories.

DECISION-MAKING STYLES

Snap Decisions

We make snap decisions in the blink of an eye or the snap of a finger. They are simple, immediate reactions to a specific event or situation.

> ### Oh, Snap!
> The family was eating dinner. Mandy, a feisty teenager, reached over to her little sister Olivia's plate and took a pickle. Olivia screamed and hit Mandy's hand with her fork. Mandy laughed and popped the pickle in her mouth.
>
> Mandy's mother yelled, "Mandy! What are you doing?"
>
> Mandy rudely responded, "What does it look like I'm doing?"
>
> "Herb!" Mandy's mother said furiously at her husband.
>
> Herb slammed his fists on the table and screamed, "*Everybody shut up!*"
>
> Olivia started to cry, and Mandy jumped up and ran from the table. Herb looked at his wife. "Now are you happy?" he asked, tossing his napkin on his plate and turning on the TV. Dinner was ruined.

In the previous scenario, you are introduced to a chain of snap decisions. Mandy taking Olivia's pickle, Olivia jabbing Mandy with the fork, Mom screaming at Mandy, Mandy giving a snippy response, Mom summoning Dad, and Dad screaming. The escalation of emotions with each snap decision culminated in what I like to call an *emotional tornado*. Emotional tornados are like real tornados, except it's the destructive power of unstable emotions, rather than wind, that wreaks havoc. The outcome is similar, though; everyone in the path of an emotional tornado is in danger.

Snap decisions are made instantaneously, without any thought to an outcome. Grocery stores count on you making snap decisions at the checkout counter; they place magazines and candy there, hoping to catch your attention and cause you, in the blink of an eye, to spend a few dollars more.

We make snap decisions more frequently when we're engaged in a distracting activity and are not as aware of our choices. The checkout counter is one example; you are there to pay for your food, but you see the candy. You saw the candy in the candy aisle, but you were focused on shopping and didn't buy the candy because it wasn't on your list. Another example is when you're playing tennis and a bee comes near you. Normally you would ignore the bee or walk away, but in the heat of the match, you swat the annoying thing and get stung. Pure reaction … no thought to consequence.

HABITUAL DECISIONS

A habit is a repeated behavior. Habitual decisions are choices we make based upon the fact that we took this action before, and so now repeating that action, with little or no thought to outcome, is our choice again.

> ### Yesterday, Today ... Probably Tomorrow, Too
> Doris and Dan were writing out their invitations to their holiday party, just as they had done for the past eight years. Dan looked at Doris and said, "Why didn't we send these as e-mails? It's so much easier and less expensive." "I don't know," Doris answered. "It never even occurred to me."

We make habitual decisions, like snap decisions, without much thought. They are non-decision decisions. An example of a habitual decision is looking at your wrist for your watch, even when you aren't wearing one. Other positive or neutral habitual decisions are brushing our teeth, getting up on the same side of the bed, or sleeping on the same side of the bed. Doing something repeatedly, in the same way, without really giving it much thought, is habitual decision-making.

POSITIVE, NEGATIVE, AND NEUTRAL HABITUAL DECISIONS

Not all habitual decision-making is positive or neutral. Some negative habits are smoking, not showering, or not wearing seat belts in the car. Negative habitual decision-making often undermines relationships. People who refuse to see what is happening in real time, who resort to relying on what always used to be, lose their ability to choose a positive outcome. Take, for instance, the mother who has a child who needs a lot of attention in elementary school but is able to move independently upon reaching middle school. The mother's caretaking identity is attached to the dependent child, and when the child becomes independent the repeated, habitual caretaking behaviors undermine their positive relationship.

A positive habitual behavior that builds a relationship could be a phrase that a partner uses in times of stress. In my house, when someone is caught up in a heated moment and spilling his or her every thought and emotion, our automatic (or habitual) response is, "Are you telling me this because you want my opinion or just because you need to vent?" This one sentence has averted many arguments. There are good and bad habitual decisions, depending on whether they lead you toward or away from your ultimate goal.

PLANNED DECISION-MAKING

Planned decision-making requires thought. It means weighing choices and anticipating outcomes. If you engage in planned decision-making, then you must have multiple alternative choices and evaluate the probable results that will ensue from each one.

> ### Planning Outcomes
> Pat had wanted to meet with the director of curriculum for the school district for months but was never able to get an appointment. The previous month, when attending a meeting for a community volunteer organization, Pat noticed that the director had joined the organization and attended the meeting. This month, before the meeting, Pat put together a folder and included a contact sheet. At the end of the meeting, Pat approached the director, engaged him in a conversation, and was able to give him the proposal.

Planned decisions are based upon choices that calculate probable outcomes. For example, you are considering a career change from retail sales to something that provides you with more independence. You write out four careers that you find interesting: teaching, entrepreneurship, human resources, nursing. For each of your choices, you write down how much time you will need to get the proper certifications or financial backing. You calculate the benefits of each and the possible drawbacks. You prioritize what is important to you and then evaluate which of the four careers best fits your lifestyle and also moves you toward your ultimate goal of increased independence.

ACTION VS REACTION

Decision-making is nothing new. Some decisions have positive outcomes while others—well, let's just say they have not-so positive outcomes. To increase the chances of getting a desired outcome, *you need to know what you want to have happen next.* As simple as that may seem, many of us still refuse to clarify what exactly we really want to have happen, or we deny ourselves the motivation by using the undermining alibi "I am not in control of what happens next."

For most of us, denying ourselves the right to choose what we want to happen next is actually more common then identifying an achievable outcome. This denial route allows us to *choose* the easy way out—choosing to *re*act to the situation. Consider the word *react*—act again. It usually means to fall into a habitual behavior, with little thought to the actual behavior or the consequences it will bring about. We unconsciously, or sometimes habitually, decide to continue choosing behaviors that have been demonstrated to not work. Other times we jump into a tempting new choice through a snap decision, again with no thought to its consequences. When behaviors miss the goal, complaints of running out of luck or being a victim of fate are not far behind. Sometimes, in desperate situations, we might even blame our failure to achieve a personal goal on the lack of an able rescuer! You know the line: "if only so and so had been there to help." The problem with all these excuses is that they don't allow us the time to consider that *the consequences we are living with are a direct result of the fact that when the opportunity for self-determination was a choice, we decided to ignore it.*

So if we choose not to engage in planned action, whether due to habitual procrastination or a feeling of helplessness, the outcome of feeling victimized is the end result. Like it or not, we are both the victim and the victimizer.

> **MARSHALL'S LAW #3:** Refusing to make a choice *is* making a choice.

SUMMARY

Becoming who you want to be, creating the life you want to live, demands that you make choices that will lead you in the right direction. There are three types of decision- making: snap, habit, and planned. Snap and habit are easy outs, ways to react to the circumstances around you rather than choosing to move in your positive direction. Snap and habitual decisions move the energy to create what happens next out of your hands. Only planned decision-making, or choosing from multiple actions with awareness of consequence, will keep the energy to make what you want to have happen next actually occur. The only benefit of emotional reaction is the built-in excuse of emotional negligence it provides you when things go terribly wrong.

CHAPTER 5

WHAT IS CHANGE?

CHANGE

The word *change* can be used as a verb—to change, indicating an action describing an alteration of something—or a noun that describes coins and loose money. It can be given as a command ("Change your shirt!") or to demonstrate reflection ("I've changed my mind"). The action can be as concrete and measurable as the change in temperature or as elusive as a change of heart. A primary, constant, and important fact to remember though, is that there is no such thing as small change.

Consider the pennies you have lying around—what we call "loose change." Even those pennies can become a million dollars. It all depends on what you choose to do when you find pennies in your pocket. If you're consistent in putting your change in a jar, within a matter of time you will see changes that you can bank on. On a yearly basis, my family and I take a vacation where the spending money (sometimes several hundred dollars' worth) comes from our penny jar.

So what has this got to do with your ability to achieve your goal of happiness?

Everything! Accumulating small increments of change pays off from a behavioral standpoint as well. In this age of instant media gratification, we have begun to buy into the idea that big changes are the only ones that count. We think we can lose fifteen pounds in a week and keep it off or that we can go online and find a life partner in six months (money-back guarantee!). The media has convinced us that if we want something badly enough, we can almost will it into being. How many of us have watched an exercise program on TV and thought that by watching the exercise we were somehow engaging in the behavior? It's time for a clarification of terms, if you're going to become who you wanted to be.

BEHAVIOR AND BEHAVIOR CHANGE

Behavior translates into action—something you *do*, physical acts that you can see and measure. Behavior is concrete. It's not about thinking or dreaming or hoping or wishing. Behavior change is not about just changing how you think of something; it's about your actions. Behavior change is the alteration of specific actions.

> **MARSHALL'S LAW #4:** Despite popular belief, **wishing and hoping are not courses of action!**

The smallest change in your behavior often affects not only your immediate environment and personal life, but also the lives of those around you and future events for all involved. Behavior is about how "human doings" can affect human beings. An old children's folk song called "Found a Peanut" perfectly explains this phenomena. A child finds a peanut that is rotten and decides to eat it anyway. The child then gets sick, the doctor comes, and in my childhood version, the child dies. Many other childhood rhymes have the same theme; they are methods for teaching children how to make better decisions. In our politically correct society, many of these songs have been censored because they're considered violent or disturbing. As a result, their messages have been left unsaid. The "Found a Peanut" song demonstrates that although the child just picks up the rotten peanut and eats it, the consequences involve the family and the medical system, and they ultimately end the child's life. All because of one small act. An action. A behavior.

Every action you take affects the direction of your life and the people who you have invited into your living circle. For this reason, each one of us needs to think carefully about our choices and the behaviors we decide to engage in, the behaviors we think we should engage in, and the behaviors we will ultimately decide to extinguish (or do no more).

YOUR BEHAVIOR

Consider your home-base behavior, the one you will be working on. Here are some important questions you might want to ask yourself: How did I decide upon this behavior? Was it a snap, habitual, or planned decision?

It's time to turn up your "insight volume" to amplify your decision-making processes. By being more mindful of choices you are making, you can elect to engage in behaviors that move your life in the direction you want to go. Your insight volume places you in the driver's seat, actively navigating your path, rather than reacting to your arrival.

It's important to be in tune with the decisions you have made so far, the ones that have brought you to the place you find yourself in now. Every choice you have made in your life has brought you to this moment. Through developing a heightened awareness of your past behaviors, you will increase your ability to be aware of not only your present behaviors and their impact on your future, but also the behaviors of those around you and how *their* choices impact *your* life. As you identify your snap and habitual choices, and either eliminate them or reinforce them, you will begin to predict, with more agility, the choices that will lead you where you want to go.

MARSHALLS LAW #5: You are responsible for the life you have right now. **Every choice you have made, up to and including today, has created the life you lead at this moment.**

PREDICTING BEHAVIOR CHANGE

Since humans appeared on this Earth, the skill or ability to adapt and adjust to changing environments has always been the determining factor for survival. I'm happy to report that humans are able to thrive on change. The question we need to ask ourselves is this: how did we cognitively learn how to adapt?

For most of us, adaptation occurs on a subconscious level; it's not something we think about all the time. We observe and remember (or write down) the event, keeping a mental or verbal account of what happened. We might notice that when one event occurs, a second event usually follows. For example, the sun rises in a clear sky and then there is light, or clouds fill the sky and then rain falls. These contingent events (the second event requires the first to occur) make us able to develop predictions.

Human behavior is usually based upon either innate reaction (instinct) or a learned response. A baby's first breath is instinctual, not learned, as is the baby's first cry. If, however, someone comes to help each time the baby cries, the baby will learn to cry in order to get help. Innate or instinctual behavior does not use choice. It is a state of being. Learning how to repeat the behavior so that a specific outcome is achieved is a state of doing. As one of my students once said, innate behavior is "preprogrammed into our DNA," whereas learned responses and other purpose-driven behaviors involve choice.

This kind of learning, engaging in unconscious behaviors that are reinforced by the repeated consequences that occur, elicits repetitive learned responses that continue in life. We determine early on that we can choose behaviors we would like to engage in, believing that we control the outcome of those behaviors. We make these choices believing that if we do *x*, then *y* will follow. We base these predictions on our past experiences and learned knowledge. Examples of this learning can be seen with children who learn that crying gets immediate attention, that pointing at an object will draw the attention of others to that object, and that smiling at an adult will elicit a smile in return.

In medicine, this ability to predict what will happen, based upon a set of events or symptoms, is called diagnosis and treatment. In public health, the capacity to predict human behavior, based upon events and past behaviors, has led to the development of successful immunization plans and public health initiatives. It has also refined our ability to recognize barriers to behavior change, as well as methods to enhance the benefits.

Of course, living in the twenty-first century gives us a lot of choices. Life is not as simple as it was in prehistoric times. Today we have procedures for emergency preparedness, and we are acutely aware of natural and man-made disasters. When I tell my children that my teachers and parents taught me a skill called "duck and cover" and that I used to hide under my desk during an air raid drill (huh? what's that?) to avoid being vaporized by a nuclear bomb, they laugh. At the time, common knowledge and wisdom told us that what we were doing would be effective. Today, however, "duck and cover" is obsolete.

So what has changed? Information access. Now we know more about the effects of the atomic bomb and the devastation that it causes. Back then the duck-and-cover strategy was a choice of behavior based upon a theory, not a tested reality. In the time between then and now, experiences have taught us that this response would be worthless if a nuclear event actually occurred. Research shows us that the most effective human search engine is the use of the words *what, when, why,* and *how.* By questioning our environment, we can figure out our relationships with other, and choose responses to them that will increase our ability to move in the direction of our choice.[2]

It is shocking to realize that most of us still use the duck-and-cover approach in our personal lives. We choose to implement outdated and ineffectual strategies to protect our emotions and chart new directions. It's akin to navigating with only the stars as our guides, during a category five hurricane in the twenty-first century.

CHARTING THE COURSE TO WEATHER EMOTIONAL STORMS

Each day you wake up and maybe, like me, you listen to your favorite morning announcer who tells you the temperature and how it will change over the course of the day. I live in the northeast, so knowing what the day's weather will be is extremely important. I've learned the hard way that just looking out my window is insufficient for making a twenty-four-hour decision on.

In the 1980s, the meteorologists in Israel went on strike. No one was that concerned, though, because Israel, like California, enjoys a fairly predictable climate. The unpredictability of the environment increases the value of the advice of a good weatherperson. Our decisions about what to wear, how to dress our children, where to park the car, and even what to buy at the supermarket are based upon the weatherperson's prediction. Advice is valuable to others only if they respect the reliability of past performance. If each time you provide advice to someone it turns out badly for the person, he or she will not seek your advice in the future. The advisor must have more information, and that information must be reliable for it to have value to the advisee.

The science of climatology is fairly accurate, so we have faith in its predictions. Research using radar, satellites, software, and computer analysis coupled with good old observation has yielded respectful, science-based models that are reliable predictors of the weather.[3] We also know some predictions without the help of the weather bureau, because climates occur in patterns, such as the seasons, the tides, and the waxing and waning of the moon. Most of us are comfortable packing a bathing suit when we leave for the Caribbean or a winter jacket when we visit Canada in the winter. We have this level of comfort because the distance of the destination to the equator establishes the *probability* of the weather. In other words, the tropics will be hot; the northern tundra will be cold. The specific patterns of weather, such

31

as the occurrence of rain or snow, will vary depending on the atmospheric conditions at the time of the visit.

Consider now that most human actions are as predictable as the weather. Human beings have patterns of expected life passages and developmental stages. Some we have nicknames for, such as the "terrible twos" and "midlife crisis." When we are alerted to a specific stage, we prepare our responses accordingly. We expect babies to roll over at a certain age, to talk at a certain age, and to pass into adulthood by beginning puberty at a certain age. Understanding the developmental cycles of human development aids us in determining how to respond and relate to others.

Each one of us has unique, repetitive behavior patterns. As predictable as these patterns are to us and those who know us, and despite the emotional hailstorms we see outside our homes, many of us choose to go out into these tempests with no protection at all! Why is it that on almost a daily basis, some of us choose to leave home in virtual bathing suits, disregarding the windblasts of anxiety and the emotional snowdrifts outside our doors?

It is almost as though choosing to "*re*act" to the situation is the preferred course, trumping preparation, anticipation, and engagement in a planned action. Reaction opens the door to habitual and snap decision-making. Reactive decisions usually increase the barrier between you and your goal. Reaction provides instant gratification (you win the battle) but not sustainable progress to the ultimate goal (you win the war). Reactive behavior also builds in an "excuse factor" for failure.

The truth is that you are always more likely to succeed when you choose to act, rather than react. That said, sustainable success comes with grown-up responsibility. Unfortunately, life doesn't come with an owner's manual. Despite the fact that we're surrounded by "experts" who have spent their lives studying our behaviors, emotions, and collective unconscious, their interventions usually occur when we are broken or in bad need of repair.

Why wait? Why not start enjoying your life now? My experience has demonstrated that when we are able to identify what makes us happy, discover what we really want, and learn how to infuse our happiness into a portion of each day, we are able to enjoy our lives without guilt. In this way, we join hands with change and move gracefully toward our goals. That, my friends, is how a human being becomes a human doing. And that's what we need to win in this human race.

Reaction and Stagnation

Ami is working on a report that is due tomorrow. Ami's been working on it the whole day. Friends stop by and say they're going for a quick bite at the local hangout. Ami hasn't eaten all day, and the idea is appealing. Unfortunately, the report must take priority.

Ami explains that the report is the priority and rejects the offer to go out. One of Ami's friends says, "You always choose work. You used to be one of us! What's happened to you? You are turning into an old, boring person!" The group of friends laugh at the remark and make more insulting digs until they see Ami shrug her shoulders.

Without measuring the priority again, Ami grabs a jacket and a credit card and chooses to leave the report until the morning. The group has fun, and the next morning Ami's report is still not done. Ami's emotional reaction to the remarks stopped her progress toward her goal, putting the power of what happened next into the hands of her "friends."

SUMMARY

Change is the constant we all live with. The choice we have is how we choose to prepare for it and live with it. Actions we take, through the choices we make, determine whether we are basing our behaviors on reliable predictions or emotional reactions. Small, consistent planned changes can produce stable, long-lasting positive change. Even knowing this, there are still many among us who cringe at the thought of change.

CHAPTER 6

WHY CHANGE IS DIFFICULT:
THE VACUUM THEORY

What is a vacuum? It can be a machine that sucks up dirt and anything else that comes in its path, or it can be an empty void that echoes nothingness. The existence of a vacuum in an environment is destabilizing. Change causes vacuums.

> **Marshall's Vacuum Theory**: All change, positive and negative, creates loss. The loss that any change creates is a vacuum, which will be filled with whatever happens to be around at the time of the loss.

It is understandable that people repeat behaviors that lead them to their goals, but what about those behaviors that don't move people forward? Why repeat behaviors that fail to achieve the desired effect? What kind of positive effect is produced simply by repeating a behavior again and again?

The pattern of repeated behavior, not unlike a pattern of repeated weather, instills us with a sense of knowing. We glean a certain level of comfort in the repetition, and it makes us feel good to be able to forecast the next occurrence. We see clouds, we hear thunder, and either we wait and listen for the impending whistle, or we exit the swimming pool even before the lifeguard's warning. We believe that we know what is going to happen next. This sense of *knowing* empowers us, and feeling empowered makes us feel good. Even though we don't want to get out of the water, we feel somehow that we're in control; we correctly anticipated what was going to happen next.

NEGATIVE PATTERNS AND LEARNED HELPLESSNESS

Patterns, even negative ones, give us a sense of control and power. When we are placed in situations where we believe that nothing we can do will ever affect the outcome of the situation, we feel helpless. The theory of learned helplessness brings together the same elements of behavioral prediction in that there is a contingent effect of one event producing another; in other words, if I do x action, it will cause y reaction.[4] The problematic difference between behavioral prediction and learned helplessness is that the contingent (resulting) behavior for the learned helpless is uncontrollability of outcome; in other words, no matter what action I take, the same reaction will occur.

Harmful Advice and Passive Consent

Bibi was an excellent student. Before graduating, students were assigned an advisor who would oversee the final graduation project. Bibi's advisor, Pat, seemed nice and supportive on their first meeting, and Bibi began her work.

The first time Bibi brought the work to her advisor, Pat exclaimed, "This is awful! How could you possibly have gotten this far in your studies? Aren't you ashamed to turn in trash like this? I see now why they assigned you to me. We have a lot of work to do!"

Pat ripped up the pages and sat Bibi down in a chair, dictating instructions for a rewrite.

The second, third, and fourth times Bibi went to see Pat, the scene was repeated. Pat would shout insults, rip up the pages, and send Bibi back to start again. When Bibi cried, Pat showed no sympathy. "You better get it right," she said. "I am your only hope for graduation. I won't tell anyone how terrible your work is, but I will work with you so that you'll be able to graduate."

This pattern of abuse, and the threat of not graduating, convinced Bibi that her future was in the hands of Pat. When Bibi told a friend about her sessions with Pat, the friend advised her to change advisors. Bibi panicked and said that if she did, she would never graduate. After that, Bibi told no one about Pat. She continued in this pattern until one day the principal overheard one of the abusive sessions and reassigned Bibi to a different advisor.

Despite the pain Bibi associated with her negative interactions with Pat, Bibi steeled herself before each meeting, quickly learning what to expect at the sessions. Through the endurance of repeated verbal abuse, Bibi (believing herself a survivor) actually became a helpless person. She learned helplessness. A helpless person believes that once a set of events begins to unfold, his or her ability to control the outcome is reduced to zero.

Breaking Patterns and Anticipating the Vacuum

The empty space where a habitual behavior used to fit, even one that was unpleasant, leaves us feeling incomplete. We know that something's missing, and it makes us uncomfortable. If you're a smoker and you give up your cigarette after dinner because you're in a restaurant, you will probably feel that dinner is not over; the experience is not satisfying. If you decide to cut out coffee from your diet, the finishing touch to breakfast never arrives. Changing a behavior, without having a replacement behavior to fill the void, increases the probability of slipping back into the old, unwanted behavior.

The loss of the old behavior creates a vacuum. Anticipate it! Outsmart it! If you decide to go on a diet, the first thing you should do is buy healthy foods and begin to snack on them. Choose healthy food over junk food, even when junk food is available. Then when you begin your diet, remove the old food (the temptation) and place your new foods where you can easily access them. This way, when you're hit with the urge to munch on something, you have a choice of only healthy foods. It won't be as easy to slip into the old habit of ice cream and cookies.

Your Behavior

Consider for a minute your home-base behavior, and anticipate what kinds of vacuums might develop when you begin your change. Do the same for any behavior you decide to change. As soon as you know what you want to change, begin storing up alternative behaviors/actions as a replacement. Before giving up your habit, begin to decrease where and when you indulge in it. Then, when you begin to have an urge, actively choose the more positive replacement behaviors.

For example, let's look at dieting. When changing eating habits, a person has to decide to either eat less or not eat certain foods. An easy and effective method for making this change is to fill the old noshing time with a more acceptable, healthy behavior, such as taking a walk. When I want to lose some weight, I increase my intake of sparkling water. (I also found this to be effective when I quit smoking.) Drinking water satisfies my oral need, fills me up, and is good for me. I can also do it anytime and almost anywhere.

Without a plan to fill the vacuum, you may feel helpless to control the urge to return to the old way of being. When, and if, you slip back into the old behavior, you unwittingly reinforce your belief that you're unable to determine your own future. This reaction can foster a sense of learned helplessness, which then increases your likelihood toward inaction. The important word in the last sentence is "learned" helplessness. Like Bibi, you are repeating a behavior that is not moving you to your goal; in fact, it's actually a barrier toward the successful achievement of your goal. Once you begin to implement the strategies and skills of self-determined behavior, you will be able to break the cycle of learned inaction.

Self-determined behavior is a skill. Like any skill, it requires practice to become natural. Since all behavior change incurs loss, it's helpful to understand how a person defines loss. Each year I ask my students how change can be seen as loss. Year after year, everyone invariably goes to the loss of life, the loss of innocence, and the loss of a relationship. Their interpretation of change as loss is so sad. The intense kind of change and ensuing loss that my students identify is only part of the picture. There is also everyday change and everyday loss, such as changing the time you go to bed, starting a diet, or rearranging your furniture.

Change as Loss

Louis loved sameness—eating the same foods, staying in the same hotels, keeping the furniture he had from his youth. When he married Barbara, he knew she loved change, but he never anticipated that her love of change would affect his home life.

One day he came back from work to find all the furniture in their apartment rearranged. Barbara, energized and excited, greeted him with a big smile. The look on Louis's face, however, was anything but pleased.

"What have you done? I liked it the way it was!" he stammered.

"I just wanted to surprise you," she said, a bit hurt.

Louis's face reflected sadness and defeat, which gave way to concern. "You mean you did this all alone? Didn't you think that you could have gotten hurt?" He looked around the room until he saw his favorite chair, and then he pulled it back to where it used to be and slumped into it.

After a long day at work, Louis just wanted to come home to his familiar surroundings and relax. Barbara had ruined that for him by changing the position of the furniture. Because of her independent actions, Louis had lost his comfort zone. Barbara hadn't intended to make him sad, so together they put the furniture back. Barbara didn't understand that Louis, like so many of us, had faith in the familiar, which had been knocked off balance by her impulsive actions.

To some degree, we are all creatures of habit. We like our specific brands of toothpaste, our bath soaps, and our detergents. When we can't find them, or our lucky sweater, cap, or coat, we are pushed into a realm of disquiet. Usually we just trudge on with a fleeting tinge of anxiety or annoyance, and then we settle for something else. Before long, that something else becomes equally familiar.

SUMMARY

All change, no matter how small, creates a loss, which in turn creates a vacuum. The more entrenched we are with keeping the status quo, the bigger the experience of loss will be in the face of any change. Anticipating and preparing for change allows us to succeed in achieving growth, lessening the sense of loss and the instability that accompanies the vacuum.

Chapter 7

Pro Strategy: The Vacuum Antidote

When you turn on a vacuum, whatever is in the way of the suction will be sucked in. It doesn't matter whether you wanted it to go; once the vacuum is on, the object is gone. So it is with the behavior vacuum. When you change your behavior, you turn on the vacuum. Something has to fill the void. Usually what will surface is whatever was closest to your habitual behavior before the void.

It is important not to set yourself up for failure. Choosing to prepare for success means that after deciding to change your eating habits, you become vigilant about stocking the refrigerator with good foods. This decision-making action makes certain that when hunger strikes and you open that fridge door, you have only good items to choose from. You didn't tame the desire, but you managed the choices to get you to your goal.

What happens, though, when you go to a friend's home, get hungry, and open her fridge? Hmmm ... all the bad foods you've decided to forgo are back in your face. You want to eat, so what is your choice?

The vacuum antidote is based upon incremental change. Small, consistent changes need to occur over time. Once these small, almost imperceptible changes are linked together, you will find that you have taken a huge step toward your *big* change.

For example, let's stay with the goal of eating better. Start replacing foods slowly. Instead of a snacking on a candy bar, have an apple. Make sure you have healthy snacks available to munch on so that you don't go bonkers with hunger driving home after a long day at work. This way when the void occurs, what is closest to the suction is the new, much improved, goal-oriented behavior. Welcome to the "Preemptive Replacement Option," or PRO Strategy.

PRO STRATEGY

The PRO Strategy allows you to practice the behaviors you want to have, when you are *not* in the suction mode. This way, when the suction turns on, the new behaviors are already in position, saving you from falling back into old, unwanted habits. If you are hungry and you have to search for good food, you build in a perfect excuse for reverting to the old behaviors. Have you ever noticed how some people are able to anticipate their own behaviors so well that they rarely experience the negative effects of the vacuum? Watch them closely—they're probably change-partners! Consistent practice of the PRO Strategy creates positive, habitual decision-making that paves the way to your goal. Soon even you habitual choices will reflect self-determined behavior.

Self-determination is the gold standard of vacuum antidotes. It's also extremely effective against learned helplessness, chronic Bitching, Moaning and Complaining (BMCing), spasms of undermining alibi creation, and the occasional (or virulent), emotionally based snap decision.

Choosing to repeatedly engage in snap and negative, habitual decision-making, despite the certainty of negative outcomes, is the training ground for life in a perpetual vacuum. The knowledge that you have no control over your environment and the people in it, but that you *can* choose to control your response to them, is the first step toward achieving self-determined behavior.

BEATING THE LOSS VACUUM

Vacuums will occur in the natural course of your life because life is vibrant and always changing. How you choose to respond to those changes will determine the size of the vacuum. How you choose to act when faced with the vacuum will shape your future. Any strategy that you discover that keeps you focused on your goal and allows you time to think before engaging in a reaction to your environment is a vacuum antidote.

Achieving self-determined behavior is a skill. Like any skill, it requires practice to become proficient and continued practice to maintain a comfortable level of expertise. We all like immediate results and can be discouraged when the desired effect seems remote. This discouragement will lead you on a slippery slope back to your old behaviors, so take a step back and change the immediate goal. Refocus on what you want to have happen in the next ten to fifteen minutes. Then place 100 percent of your concentration into that goal. You will notice that as you work on your fifteen-minute goal, the intensity of the suction pulling you back in the direction of your unwanted behaviors will decrease.

To succeed in life, we need the three Rs: reading, 'riting, and 'rithmetic. To succeed against the suction of the loss vacuum, we need to engage in PRO Strategy and use the seven Rs.

- **Refocus:** Stop reacting to your environment, and refocus on your goal.
- **Reframe:** Change the way you see the environment/event, and deactivate your reaction button.
- **Reset/Reboot:** Find a not-too-obvious place on your body, and call it your reset button. When you start to lose control, press your reset button and reboot your emotional filter. As you press the button, say, "I am in control of my response to my environment."
- **Remove:** When all else fails, remove yourself from the environment that is sucking you back into your old behaviors.
- **Restore:** Once you are safely away from the vacuum, remind yourself what you want to accomplish and breathe. Restore your faith in yourself. You can accomplish your goal.
- **Regulate:** Remember the event and the environment that almost trapped you into the old habit. Regulate yourself by either avoiding this situation or anticipating it and preparing for it.
- **Reality Check:** Make sure you are evaluating your environment and the present situation correctly. Is your perception of what is happening based in today's reality, or is does it reflect something that happened in the past? Often a behavior is a response to what you perceive or believe to be someone else's desire to control you. The truth is that what you *believe* really does affect what you *do*. Thought and intention precedes action and can affect your response to a vacuum. When you begin to act on a perception, stop and do a reality check.

SUMMARY

Armed with the knowledge that change can ignite the vacuum, it is helpful to have strategies to resist the pull. Using the PRO Strategy (Preemptive Replacement Option) will enable you to practice substituting behaviors and change objects, prior to the actual moment of change. Consistently using the

PRO Strategy will allow you the time to slowly get accustomed to the change, without feeling the loss. When the feeling of loss does occur, you can use the seven Rs to help focus your thoughts toward moving through the vacuum to goal achievement.

CHAPTER 8

PERCEIVED CONTROL AND BEHAVIOR

Take a moment to consider what the picture below means to you. Who is in the picture? What are they doing? Which of the figures do you feel most reflects you?

Common responses from adults include:

- People have to constantly jump through hoops.
- Life is about taking orders.
- Nothing gets accomplished without someone barking orders.
- You have to yell to get compliance
- There's always a boss ready to make you do what you don't want to do.

Common responses from children include:

- People are training for the Olympics.
- It's a gym class, and the coach is helping the students.
- People are learning how to be gymnasts.
- Kids are having fun doing flips.

As you might have guessed, there are no wrong answers. Each opinion reflects the individual's interpretation and is based upon his or her past experiences and future expectations. It's the person's perception that colors the meaning.

What was your response to the picture? Did you see yourself in the role of a coach, boss, or bully, or were you a gymnast, employee, or victim? Your answer may reveal your preconceived, automatic response to giving or being given direct orders. It may also help explain your reactive behaviors.

Wherever your identity lies, take a minute to consider the opposite viewpoint. Our behaviors usually reflect our interpretation of the situation, which is based upon our past experiences (remember the weather prediction). Our interpretations are hidden in our minds, but our behaviors are concrete and observable by others. Public opinion and the reactions of others will be based on our visible, measurable actions, regardless of our invisible intentions. Once we put our actions out in the open for others to view, we have to live with the consequences that follow.

Like it or not, the first method to learn about people in our society is to watch what they do and listen to what they say. People around us evaluate our behaviors, creating their own stories of who we are and deciding where we fit into their lives. Based solely upon our behaviors, others will decide whether their relationship with us will be positive or negative, or whether it will even exist at all. All behavior has consequences. When you control your behavior, you can usually predict, create, or modify the consequences that follow.

Now look at the picture again with a new thought in your mind, regardless of which figure you identify with: how can either character be engaging in an action of strength, self-determination, and positive growth?

You are in control.

You might find this statement hard to accept. Maybe you, or someone you know, have believed that environmental forces act upon us, making us the victims of fate or happenstance. It is not uncommon to meet people who feel (and act) as though life is just a series of hoops that they are mandated to jump through. Consider for a moment that some people choose to be the jumpers, while others choose to be the directors. The important factor is not the action, but rather who is deciding to take responsibility for the action. Do you want to have control over your actions?

If you are the jumper, you are choosing to be the jumper. You, not the director, have made the decision to jump. Now, based upon this slight change in perspective, reframe the original control statement as follows:

You are in control of *yourself.*

You alone are capable of controlling your reaction to your environment. You have the choice to jump, coach, or sit on the sidelines. You can decide how to respond to people in different situations. Of course, the alternatives might require more energy than you want to expend, but the bottom line is that the choice is still yours and yours alone.

Let's refine that control statement once more, and make it one of Marshall's Laws.

> **Marshall's Law #6: You are *only* in control of your response to your environment.** When you choose to give up control of your behavioral response, either through snap or habitual decision-making, you have chosen to relinquish your control over your future. Someone else *will* step in, and your behavior has given that person permission.

Stabilization Through Self-Determination

It's time for you to engage in some self-determined behaviors—behaviors that will be a direct result of your chosen, planned actions. Experiencing consistent, self-determined behavior increases your understanding of the impact your behavior has on your environment and the people in it. You will no longer feel a victim of changing environments. Instead, you will be able to predict instability in the environment and chart a course toward stability.

Take a moment to look at your life. Are your priorities and energies spent calming day-to-day crises, or are they focused on moving you toward your life goal? Where can you choose to exert your self-control so that you can pursue your own dreams? What goals have eluded you because you've squandered your energies on the little battles of daily living and the lack of conscious, self-determined behaviors? During this informal inventory, identify the times and situations where you chose to be controlled by others, where your undermining alibis eclipsed your determination to follow your goal. There's a choice here. You can continue to allow your undermining alibis to rule your future, or you can take the reins of responsibility back into your own hands through planned action.

What can you expect as you become more self-determined?

Experiencing consistent, conscious, self-determined behavior increases your understanding of the impact you have on your environment and the people in it. You might feel like relinquishing those futile attempts to control others (such an energy waster!). Your small but constant, daily successes will mount up. You may become aware of how you used to manipulate others into thinking that they controlled you, and you may see how that too works against your capacity to achieve your own goals. This skill of convincing others—and sometimes even ourselves—that others are controlling us usually becomes the perfect excuse for our failures.

You can expect to become a kind of expert in sensing environments that are ripe for change and those that are setups for disaster. Your capacity to refrain from knee-jerk, snap decisions will empower you with a skill that will transform your emotional environment. When you feel the emotional tides begin to turn, and your own emotional emotions begin to destabilize, your automatic response will be to evaluate the situation and plan your route to safety. It will be like you have a state-of-the-art emotional environment alert system that will allow you to prepare for, and survive, even the most unstable situation.

So, how do you achieve this level of skill?

Learning a Skill

The distinguishing factor between the windsurfer who enjoys riding the challenging winds, and the one who runs to the harbor when the winds increase, is the surfer's experience and level of ability. A professional windsurfer is able to predict the wind's affect on the waves and the sail, and he or she can demonstrate a practiced skill in working with the wind. Becoming an expert takes time, experience, and consistent practice. It means starting in calm, safe, protected waters, where the surfer can perfect balance issues before adding the additional challenge of the wind.

Successful change-partners practice achieving emotional balance in calm times, which prepares them for riding out more challenging situations. Engaging in self-control and experiencing the increased predictability of outcomes that accompanies it, can produce a high of sorts. This exhilaration reflects the self-satisfaction one receives from successfully finishing a challenging race or being recognized for a job well done.

In order to practice the skills of self-determination, boundary setting is imperative.

Setting Boundaries

As a starting point, practice the following statements as often as possible over the next few weeks or months.

- "No."
- " I'll need some time to think about that."
- "I'm not comfortable sharing that information right now."

The next time your mother asks you to pick up your cousin from the airport, or your partner asks whether you think your future together is bright, or even when someone simply asks you what you want for dinner, use one of the aforementioned statements. It's a funny experiment, but you'll notice that using one of these three statements will help you begin to feel comfortable setting (or resetting) some basic boundaries. You will have control over what *you* want to have happen next, as well as building in the time to choose action over reaction. Most enjoyably, you will have the comfort of knowing that you are responsible only for your own actions. Believe me when I say, that is *more* than enough.

SUMMARY

Self-determination employs planned decision-making in order to actively achieve desired outcomes. Prioritizing what *you* want to have happen next, and focusing your energy on each step that brings you closer to your goal, strengthens your ability to achieve success.

CHAPTER 9

HARD FACTS AND BELIEF BUFFERS

Hard fact: a fact that is real, concrete, and indisputable.

For example: all life ends in death.

A primary hard fact understood by all change-partners is that none of us are in control of what happens next. We can, however, choose to be in control of how we respond to what happens next. That, in turn, might influence what happens after that.

Of course, some of you still won't believe me. You might say that you know people who do control what happens next. Other people who panic at the thought of change—the change-aphobes—will desperately cling to their snap decisions with jaws-of-death strength, screaming that it is precisely because of our lack of environmental control that we are forced to react without planning. The "I told you so" change-aphobes will counter with "Even when we carefully plan for things to occur, and we act in a way that should reasonably make them happen, something unwanted and often undesirable occurs. Then what?"

I feel your panic, but take a deep breath and reduce the emotional noise in your head. If you're frightened by what I say, you are on the verge of change. Change is loss, and loss is scary—that is, until you understand that where you are headed is better than where you have been or even where you are now.

Okay, breathe … in through the nose, out through the mouth.

Here's a *hard fact:* you are not in control of anyone else. You are not in control of your environment. These are variables that we sometimes like to believe that we control (such as a partner, a child, or a classroom), but in reality, the only thing we can control is our reaction to the partner, child, or classroom. When we control our actions, we often impact what will happen next.

Fact: bad things happen to people who are nice, who do good deeds, and who act with kindness and good will.

Fact: good things happen to people who are really rotten, who do bad deeds, and who live to make the lives of others miserable.

You have no control over these facts.

THE BMC CLUB

So how do we deal with these harsh facts? Some of us have developed undermining alibis for the way things are. They allow us to blame another entity, or fate, or something else besides ourselves.

Of course there's always the BMC (Bitch, Moan, and Complain) Club. It would be unfair to overlook those of you who have signed up for lifelong memberships! After all, this behavior has served many people very well for the majority of their years on Earth. BMCers identify one another in a crowd, gathering with kindred spirits to partake in group absolution. BMCers are notorious for refusing to be accountable for their choices and actions. Everyone knows at least one BMCer, and we have all joined the club at least once in our lifetimes.

When a BMCer leaves the club and becomes a positive change-partner, choosing action over reaction and planned decisions over snap or habitual ones, he or she finds a whole lot less to BMC about! Notice I said less—not nothing. A good BMCer can, and most likely will, always find something.

Warning! Belonging to the BMC Club can become addictive. When you choose reaction or inaction, things rarely turn out the way you want them to. A BMCer will concentrate on the negative aspects of any situation, not understanding that what you concentrate on becomes your reality. What you look for is what you find! It's the old "don't look at my nose" trick (revisit chapter one if you don't remember).

So for those of us who prefer to see the positive potentials of each situation, we usually are able to manipulate or manufacture positive outcomes. I say *usually* because it's not always possible. Life is not consistent or predictable, and sometimes getting stuck in a bad thought can halt all our progress.

BELIEF BUFFERS

This inconsistency between what we are told to expect from life and what really happens is sometimes just too much to bear. As a result, we hold onto our "belief buffers." A belief buffer is a thought that we hold onto that helps us weather difficult moments. Whether real or not, belief buffers soften the blow of emotional hardship and give us hope (despite all real indicators) that somewhere, somehow, in the bigger picture, things will work out. My optimistic students usually say "No good deed goes unrewarded," while my pessimistic students will retort with "No good deed goes unpunished." Both, however, know that many good deeds are rewarded, while others, unfortunately, do not result in happy endings.

Belief buffers help us cope during hard moments. Like pacifiers, they soothe our souls. We need them when we feel insecure, and without them we are like babies without our blankies. Not a pretty sight!

Why do adults need soothers? After all, every day we wake up, tense every muscle and nerve in our body, get out of bed, and attack another day. Right? We carry yesterday and all the days before that on our backs like an elephant carrying the weight of the Taj Mahal—only no one else sees it. People pass us, oblivious to our past ups and downs, and casually ask, "So, how're doin'? What's up?"

Those of us without belief buffers usually tell everyone exactly how we're doing, only to find out that not many people really want that level of detail! Often it is our level of anxiety that keeps us from being able to engage in using a belief buffer, not realizing that a simple, short-term belief buffer might be what we need to disengage from our anxiety.

Anxiety and the Belief Buffer

Mrs. M. had a child with a learning disability. Her child was in a public school where the assistant principal degraded, berated, and punished the child on a daily basis. When Mrs. M. became aware of the problem, she went to the school and explained the situation. Rather than being corrected, it escalated, with daily phone calls and threatening letters as well as in-school and out-of-school detentions for the child.

Each time Mrs. M. tried to rectify a problem, the abuse increased. Her husband joined the crusade. Soon the family, except for the child, whose disability made her unaware of the problem, was an emotional mess. Pleas to the principal and the Department of Special Services went unheard. Letters stating that there were no problems were sent to the family.

With one month of school left, Mrs. M. developed a belief buffer of "I can do anything for one month." Each day she made an action plan to support her child and ignore the school. The family's home life was restored to normal for the last month of school, and the child was moved to a new school during the subsequent year.

Belief buffers differ from BMCs, excuses, and undermining alibis in that they give us a short burst of courage and strength to pursue our course of action during times of great stress. We can fit belief buffers into our action plans by focusing our energies on answering this question: "What do *I* want to have happen next?"

YOUR CHOICE: ACT OR REACT?

When you choose to react, you are no longer driving with your hands on the steering wheel. You are concentrating on what you *don't* want to have happen next. When you decide to concentrate on what you don't want to have happen, you are actually concentrating on your resistance to change, not on the change itself. What you resist will be what persists. So your belief buffer must provide you with the positive energy to help you determine your existing choices and their likely outcomes.

Here are some belief buffer statements:

- "I can do anything for fifteen minutes."
- "The next fifteen minutes are the most important of my life. I will use them wisely."

- "I can't change what has happened, but I can work toward what I want to have happen next."

Here are belief buffer statements from some famous people.

- Dolly Parton—"Find out who you are, and do it on purpose."
- Jesse Jackson—"If my mind can conceive it, and my heart can believe it, I know I can achieve it."
- William James—"Believe that life is worth living, and your belief will help create the fact."
- Oprah Winfrey—"Breathe. Let go. And remind yourself that this very moment is the only one you know you have for sure."
- Mohammed Ali—"I figured that if I said it enough, I would convince the world that I really was the greatest."

As you develop your own belief buffers, ask yourself a few questions. With planned decision-making comes the need to plan. Planning is always best accomplished when there is little to no turmoil interrupting your thoughts. So if no pressing emotional crises are whipping up the winds of anxiety at this time, take a moment to ask yourself the following questions.

- What do I want to achieve in the next week, month, year, or five years?
  - What small steps can I take to get there?
  - What am I doing now to get there?
  - What are my choices and their possible outcomes?

If you are presently caught in the undertow of an emotional crisis, find your footing and then ask yourself the following questions.

- Now that I've uncovered this problem, is it a permanent or transient problem?
  - If I think that it's permanent, do I have more time to figure out how to deal with it?
  - If I think that it's transient, is it mandatory that I resolve this problem toward what I consider a just end, or can I live with it until I'm out of this emotional tornado?

We can fit belief buffers into our action plans by clarifying an immediate, desired outcome. Ask yourself what you want to have happen next. The question alone might be enough to help you reestablish your footing and remove yourself from the emotional undertow.

Once you are in a more stable emotional environment, ask yourself the following questions:

- What are my choices and their outcomes?
- Is this a permanent or transient problem?

Asking yourself these questions will allow you to focus on what you want to have happen next and to choose the best method of dealing with the problem at hand. It will help you choose which belief buffer might be useful to help you live with the problem while you work on the solution.

SUMMARY

You are responsible for the life you have created. Taking no action is a choice that may have real consequences. Giving others permission to choose for you is your choice, and that too has consequences. Choosing to react will shift the center of power that determines what happens next out of your hands. Determining what you want to have happen next and acting on it with a plan has consequences as well—you become responsible. Your ability to see what you want to have happen next, coupled with your planned actions, can change the course of your life toward the goal you want to achieve.

Chapter 10

Emotional Tornadoes

We talked about the predictability of the climate and the development of the science of climatology. Extreme emotions are similar to extreme weather. If we don't prepare for them, are unable to read the environmental signs that forecast them, or refuse to take shelter when they occur, we find ourselves in dire situations.

Tornadoes are a result of atmospheric instability. Stability exists when there is balance and consistency. Stable environments are reliable, dependable, and predictable.

In any unstable, tornado-like situation, whether it relates to weather or our emotions, the only goal is to get to safety. Once you are caught in a tornado, you have lost your power to make planned decisions. Unstable environments place you in harm's way at such a fast pace that you will only have access to snap or habitual decisions.

> **MARSHALL'S LAW #7: Emotional tornadoes are never worth the thrill of the ride!** Preparation in advance is the only antidote. Once you're on the ride, you have chosen reaction over action. Your control over your ability to act is gone. *Get to safety before making any major decisions!*

PREDICTING EMOTIONAL TORNADOS

Just as with the weather, emotional tornadoes sometimes allow us a lot of time to prepare and sometimes only a few seconds. As with the climate threat, the only good defense is a well thought-out offense. People swept up by an emotional tornado will give warning signs through their facial expressions, body language, and open responses to others. Watch for that internal warning system that shouts "Uh-oh, something is about to happen here that is not good!"—even though many of us have learned to ignore it.

Children who grow up in an emotionally dysfunctional household— one that had an alcoholic parent or a family member with a chronic mental illness, for example—learn to expect and live with emotional tornadoes. They see the turmoil as normal, so they don't naturally shy away from it. They are not taught that these emotionally charged situations are dangerous. They might feel terror in the pit of their stomachs, but they are repeatedly taught to accept the tornadoes as normal.

Some children think that they can lessen the impact of the tornado by causing a distraction or ignoring it. They grow into adults with little understanding of emotional survival skills. As adults, they need to learn that *they have no control over the tornado.* Getting to a safe place is their only hope of emotional survival.

There are many adults among us who remember the fear of the imminent tornado and who now find that their emotional survival skills need some reinforcement. Following are some survival strategies for living in emotional Tornado Alley.

- Know the warning signs. Don't ignore them. Get out at the first sign of a tornado. Remove yourself physically, if possible.
- If you find yourself in an environment where you are not directly part of the tornado, make a planned decision to get as physically far from the unstable person as possible. Identify (in advance) a place that could give you shelter (a bathroom, for example). Do not engage in a conversation with the unstable person. Get to a stable environment where you will be able to control your actions and stay safe.
- If you feel yourself being swept up by an emotional tornado, get away from others; they will only fan your instability. Go for a run or a walk, take a shower, or sing at the top of your lungs.

BELIEF BUFFERING AS A SHORT-TERM STRATEGY

Belief buffering is a short-term strategy that facilitates movement past an emotional barrier or insult; it is not a strategy to cope with ongoing emotional instability. Habitual belief buffering supports a persistent tornado situation by setting up the unrealistic scenario of a victim waiting to be rescued. This is frequently the defense abused women use, focusing on the arrival of help rather than developing a plan of action. In a tornado, your only thought must be to get to a safe place. Once safe, you can engage in belief buffering if needed.

Disasters do not happen only once. They occur globally on an ongoing basis. We have terrorists, anarchists, global warming, pandemic flu, and unstable financial markets. We have no control over our environment or the people in it. What the twenty-first century has taught us is that our outcome will be directly related to our "preparedness response." In other words, how we choose to behave in the disaster situation will have a direct impact on the short- and long-term effects the disasters will have on us as individuals and communities. Emotional disasters are no different.

RULES FOR RESPONDING TO EMOTIONAL DISASTERS

Just as there are rules and standards that increase our ability to respond to natural and man-made disasters, there are rules for responding to emotional disasters. By following these rules, you increase your chance of being able to weather the disaster, if not avoid it altogether.

- Be aware of your emotional environment.
- Have a plan of action.
- Get to a safe place.
- Decide what you want to have happen next, and act upon that.
- Watch what you eat and drink. Some food and beverages (caffeine, alcohol, and sugar, to name a few) will decrease you capacity to control your actions.
- *Act,* don't *react* to the situation around you.

SUMMARY

Emotional tornadoes occur when extreme emotions ignite reactive behaviors. The volatility of the situation destabilizes everyone in that emotional environment. As with the weather-related tornado, the only safe plan is to have easily accessible, planned actions that will lead you out of the path of the immediate danger. Know how to get yourself to a safe, emotionally stable place before making any important decisions.

CHAPTER 11

IMMEDIATE EMOTIONAL ENVIRONMENT (IE2) AND MEMORIES

I have come to a frightening conclusion.
I am the decisive element in my classroom.
It is my personal approach that creates the climate.
It is my daily mood that makes the weather.
As a teacher I possess tremendous power to make a child's life miserable or joyous.
I can be a tool of torture or an instrument of inspiration.
I can humiliate or humor, hurt or heal.
In all situations, it is my response that decides whether a crisis
will be escalated or de-escalated, and a child humanized or de-humanized.

—Dr. Haim G. Ginott (1976) <u>Teacher and Child</u>

ADJUSTING EMOTIONAL ENVIRONMENTS

Dr. Ginott reveals how a teacher's action and behavior toward a student determines the emotional environment for learning. Just as the ability to accurately predict the weather allows us to dress appropriately, knowing what to expect from our emotional environment empowers us to properly prepare ourselves for reasonable eventualities. During a period of emotional instability, people who are unprepared and reactive, whether they are teachers, friends, or even family members, will make everyone's lives miserable. These people are just too unpredictable to be around.

Attitudes and behaviors are to our emotional environment what atmospheric and geologic conditions are to our physical environment.

When our ability to forecast changes in the atmosphere is on target, we are more capable of engaging in action that delivers positive outcomes. Take a snowstorm, for instance. Some people will ignore the signs, scoff at the weather report, and pretend that fate will help them out. Others will choose to join (or renew) membership in the BMC Club and spend their time complaining rather than planning. This strategy doesn't produce a positive outcome, but it might eliminate the guilt associated with choosing inaction in the face of disaster (Who would've thought *that* could happen?). One thing is for certain: we can't stop snowstorms, but we *can* deal with them in a number of ways. Emergency preparedness and disaster management are two fields that have demonstrated that realistic preparation and planned actions can reduce a disaster's negative impact on our daily activities.

EMOTIONAL EMERGENCY PREPAREDNESS

Emergency preparedness is built upon the foundation of developing contingency plans that follow the logic: when x occurs, it can produce multiple other problems, such as w, y, and z. So, if x happens, I can take steps 1, 2, 3, 4, and 5 to resolve or mitigate the problem and the consequences of x through z. The key to successful emergency preparedness is in anticipating multiple possible outcomes.

Take our snowstorm, for example. The snow alone could affect our ability to commute to work, get food, keep warm, and communicate with others. Now think of how the people who shovel the roads will get to work, how the food will get to the stores, or how the doctors/nurses/ambulance drivers will get to the hospital and the patients. We can close the school, but who will make sure that the roof doesn't cave in under the snow or that the boiler doesn't burst? The level of debilitation and helplessness will be directly related to our level of preparedness for the snowstorm. In turn, the level of preparedness will be directly related to our ability to forecast reliable information.

With emotional disaster situations, many of our emotional forecasting systems lack reliable methods for predicting the effects of emotionally charged situations, leaving us without a well-developed contingency plan. This is especially true of adult children from emotionally unstable homes. As adults, these individuals often revert to behaving as they did as children, engaging in actions such as blaming, hiding, or ignoring facts—strategies that were developed to protect a child, not steer an adult.

When we know there will be a snowstorm, we can develop multiple contingency plans on both the individual level and the community level (your tax dollars at work clearing snow and reaching those with medical and utility emergencies). On an individual level, we can buy food, stock up on firewood, get a shovel, fill our tanks with gas, put chains on our tires, make sure we have enough medications for a week, and reschedule our appointments, or we can get out of town and fly south for the duration. Of course, the latter choice requires a financial solvency and independence that not many can afford. However, the senior American's choice to relocate to warmer climates after retirement is a form of long-term contingency planning. It is based upon the knowledge that advancing age makes all weather-related inconveniences, to say nothing of disaster situations, even more life threatening. Whatever the planned action, it is the negative effects of the blizzard, not the blizzard itself, that can be reduced and a positive outcome negotiated through planning and action based upon the weather forecast.

PREPAREDNESS AND IMMEDIATE EMOTIONAL ENVIRONMENTS

So how does this connect with Immediate Emotional Environments (IE2)?

Each one of us has emotional responses and actions (some snap, habitual, and planned) that we engage in during an emotional disaster. These responses are more often than not based upon gathered and stored memories of experiences and feelings. Examples of these kind of reactions can be found in the stories of disaster survivors.

Igniting Stored Memories

Marvin, a thirty-something, even-tempered, mild-mannered Louisiana native who worked as biochemist, lived in New Orleans and survived Hurricane Katrina. Shortly thereafter, he and his wife and three children relocated to Vermont and settled into a much lower-paying university position in a newly built facility.

During the fall, a rain-soaked nor'easter hit the east coast. Marvin's new building experienced some leaking, with puddles of water pouring into his office. Marvin panicked, drove home to his family at the height of the storm, and was unable to return to work without therapeutic intervention.

The level of Marvin's response to the storm reflected a post-traumatic snap response, based upon his memory of Katrina, despite the fact that the nor'easter wasn't life threatening. His actions, however, were just the opposite; at a time when he needed to think clearly, Marvin's actions increased his risk for bodily harm.

MEMORIES

Have you ever reminisced with family members or good friends about a shared event, only to realize that apart from the date and the location, each of you appeared to have totally unique memories of it? You may have even felt as though you were speaking of different events because the memories were so dissimilar! Memories are made up of specific experiences colored by thoughts that we have at the moment of the event. What turns into a memory is the specific thought, image, and feeling we chose to concentrate on at the time of the occurrence. If we choose to be with people who keep directing our attention to negative aspects of the event, more likely than not our memory will be negative as well. Events that frighten us or make us feel anxious also surface as the ones we most easily recall. They overshadow the good times because they require us to "escape" from the perceived harm. It is as though the memory has the power to trigger our old "habitual" self-defense actions, even though the present situation might not be harmful at all.

As with Marvin, our "disaster" memories frequently surface unexpectedly, blindsiding us and acting like a kind of undertow that pulls us back into irrational, snap behaviors and feelings. This emotional undertow stimulates the vacuum response. Then, we demonstrate the least stable emotional reaction closest to the suction.

At precarious moments, we most likely call upon stressful responses, even the ones that are unsuccessful, simply because they are there and are easily accessed. Why does this happen? How is it that we overcome so much, just to be sucked back into the ineffective responses of our recent or sometimes distant past? The answer lies in the way the memory triggers physical symptoms of anxiety that we want to dispel. The easiest way to do this is to engage in the habitual behavior you used to do, which initially will feel comfortable but strategically will transport you back into old behaviors that no longer fit into your life. In the following example, Tyrone experienced just such triggers each time he got together with his family for holidays.

Emotional Family Undertow

Forty-something Tyrone, married with three kids, a mortgage and a dog, was a survivor of a divorced, alcoholic family. During his twenties, Tyrone made a concerted effort to refrain from drinking, and he attended Al-Anon meetings, as did one of his six siblings. Tyrone met his wife, a nondrinker, when serving in the army. He told her of the experiences of his youth and about his desire to raise a healthy family. When their tours of duty were over, the couple decided to move to a different state and see Tyrone's family only twice a year at holidays. Tyrone made a good living and loved his family. In all aspects of his life, he considered himself a success, as did all his colleagues at work.

However, each year around the holidays, Tyrone would begin to feel anxious. His siblings and parents would call him to make plans for the visit. Normally he did not drink alcohol, but as the time for family gatherings grew near, his anxiety would peak. He would start small arguments with his spouse and kids, and he would retreat with an occasional beer. If his wife or children asked him not to drink, he'd respond angrily, "It's not illegal to have a little beer now and again, you know!"

Finally, upon reaching the family-based event, Tyrone would leave his wife and kids and join his parents and siblings, drinking and often ignoring or making jokes about his wife and kids. Within a half-hour, Tyrone would revert to behaviors he had as a teenager, totally alienating himself from his wife and children, while basking in the love and acceptance of his parents and siblings.

Very often it would take weeks to repair the damage this behavior would cause to Tyrone's relationships with his wife and children. Despite the reliability of the occurrence, every year Tyrone would promise that the next time would be different, insisting that holidays had to be spent with his family.

Tyrone kept his childhood memories under control until he got close to the family of his youth. With them, his ticket of acceptance was his uncontrolled emotional swings and ignited childhood memories. Together they created new memories that supported and normalized the validity of the old and familiar. At the same time, they altered his comfort level with his present life. Tyrone's choice to go back every year and reenact his childhood experiences fortified his old memories and responses, making permanent change difficult, if not impossible.

Tyrone was able to change his established, family-accepted behavior when he was not around them. Unfortunately, his newly chosen behaviors were demonstrated to be unreliable when he was back in the old environment. By reverting back to his old behaviors, Tyrone actually reinforced them, strengthening the probability of sliding back into them each time the family got together.

PEER PRESSURE FROM A DYSFUNCTIONAL SOCIAL GROUP

Whenever we are changing our behaviors, the act of trying on the old behavior every now and again makes it more difficult to allow the new behavior to take hold. This is because we experience an unspoken initial feeling of comfort when we revert to old behaviors. We are most susceptible to this when we are reunited with old family and friends, many of whom still see us in the persona of our youth. However, it is unhealthy when families need to make an adult child conform to old, outdated, and negative behaviors and images for the adult child to feel accepted. When this happens, it's not about the individual; it's about the mob mentality of a dysfunctional unit.

This same mob mentality or *peer pressure* phenomena can occur at work when an individual climbs the corporate ladder, leaving others he or she has worked with behind. Those unable to move up may become a dysfunctional social group. Their response to their peer advancing in the corporation turns ugly. Suddenly *workplace friends* turn their backs, and it feels as though the person getting ahead is reminded of every wrongdoing and error by those left behind. The desire to keep a group member from leaving and getting a better life may stem from the group's desire to keep the status quo, or just to remain in BMC mode, complaining about how impossible it is to get ahead. When one of them breaks from the pack, their alibi for personal mediocrity or even failure is exposed.

SHORT-TERM, LONG-TERM, EXPLICIT, AND IMPLICIT MEMORIES

How we store and recall memories can impact how we respond to them. Short-term memories are the immediate ones that we store and then access—like phone numbers and grocery lists. They are put away, taken out, and quite often lost before retrieval even occurs. Long-term memories are the ones that we store in our hard drive, and they gain permanence as part of our history. As we age and lose our capacity for short-term memories, we lean more and more on our long-term memories for personal comfort and self-identification. Explicit memory refers to the facts that we store and then access. These give us the capacity to tell a story based on facts and concepts in a coherent way. Implicit memories are the ones that we store in our muscles and other automatic response systems. It is through these implicit memories that our trigger responses are engaged. A conditioned response, like associating the smell of apple pie with Thanksgiving dinners, is stored in implicit memory.[6] Negative and traumatic events are often found in our implicit memory, with a smell, sound, or vision of some aspect of the trauma capable of kindling the full memory and the physical response associated with it.

SURVIVING EMOTIONAL OR PHYSICAL ABUSE

In situations where emotional or physical abuse is a factor, the dysfunctional group may be keeping a family secret. For example, a family living with addiction might want to keep it from neighbors and friends. The addiction (alcoholism, drug use, gambling) almost becomes a member of the family, and this family secret becomes the glue that solidifies the malfunctioning members. When one person attempts to get healthy, it destabilizes the emotional environment. The individual who has been able to begin the successful metamorphosis toward health presents a threat to keeping that secret. The rest of the family might actually sabotage the member who is disrupting the status quo. In this situation, with so much at stake, the healthy member needs to look outside the family unit for support. Any time your emotional environment contains intense pressure, anxiety, fear, and a history of maltreatment or abuse, it is best to get professional help to deal with the past and help disengage the vacuum.

REVIVING OLD MEMORIES

What is the draw, then, in reminiscing? Memories of the good old days can accentuate our best moments, and going back is an attempt to rekindle those moments. It's comforting to see people who knew and shared in our history, including many of our sorrows and joys. Sometimes, however, the memories of those moments have altered so much over time that before you know it, the gathering becomes more of a roast than a toast. Your long-term memories clash with those of your family and friends, and a pleasant walk down memory lane can become an out-of-control car chase. At those times, it's hard to accept that although you love your family members, you do not always like the way they behave. Sometimes you'll discover that you actually disapprove of how family members continue to treat you, but you don't know how to change it. Whether your reunion is a disaster or a delight, one strategy that is helpful is being honest with yourself—honest about what you want to achieve in going and honest about why you place such importance on family members liking you.

On a great Web site called StoryPeople (www.storypeople.com), the writer Brian Andreus is able to highlight critical insights about families in only a sentence or two. I always surf over to the family section where I have learned two of my methods for keeping family visits genial. One is to get together with my family, revive the memories, and leave before the volcano erupts, and the other is to pretend that they are someone else's family and that you are only there for a good (and short) visit.

SUMMARY

To be prepared for an emotionally unstable situation, you will need to be able to identify the warning signs, both from the environment and your own body. Your ability to weather the emotional tornado will be directly linked to your capacity to have a plan of action. When you understand that your memories can ignite behaviors that could further destabilize the situation, you need to have alternate behaviors ready to engage in. As you grow and change and choose self-directed, planned behaviors, you will be able to engage in relationships with family, friends, and partners that are more stable and satisfying. It also helps to keep a sense of humor!

Chapter 12

The Pig Pen Theory

To understand the impact of our memories and the automatic emotional responses they can trigger, I've developed the Pig Pen Theory of Immediate Emotional Environment (IE2).

PEANUTS © United Feature Syndicate, Inc.

Look at Charles Schulz's character, Pig Pen. Notice that cloud of dust and dirt around his feet? It's his own little sandbox that he carries with him always. Little Pig Pen always appears to be happy. When he's with his friends, the Peanuts group, his personal sandstorm doesn't bother anyone. We smile when we see Pig Pen with his cloud of dust, Linus with his blanket, and Schroeder with his little piano; their behavior-laden caricatures ignite our emotional response to little boys. When we see Pig Pen with his arms outstretched and his face beaming with a smile, the positive memories we have of "normal" little boys—cute babies who and innocently play at being pirates and firefighters—displaces the natural aversion we have to the dirt Pig Pen carries with him.

Now take a photo of your face, and place it over the face of Pig Pen.

Look carefully at that picture. What is your response when *you* are Pig Pen? Now, imagine that rather than dirt swirling around your feet, each little speck represents a memory of an event and your emotional response to that memory. Each step you take, each new environment you pass through, mixes your past and present experiences, memories, and emotions. You are constantly adding new experiences and memories, changing the cloud along the way by altering some existing memories and deleting some old ones. The memories you keep refreshing through repetition and recall are the ones that will continue to travel with you.

This emotionally charged dust cloud is what makes up a person's Immediate Emotional Environment (IE2). Like Pig Pen, our friends and family might tolerate our "dust," making us comfortable with it even in public. All too often, however, we forget that imposing our emotional dust storms on other people's environments can ruin relationships and end friendships before they even begin. Adults who have survived chaotic childhoods might feel comfortable in environments that support emotional storms, such as courtrooms and emergency rooms. Or they might veer in the opposite direction and be unable to weather emotional storms of any type.

What happens to us when we enter a place that is filled with new people—people who have their own emotional dust storms? The answer is unique to each of us. Your answer will provide you with information about the seriousness with which you view becoming who you could have been. Many of our past events have constructed the present barriers that keep us from achieving our dreams. Embracing those barriers will impede your ability to go forward. Here are some things to think about as you discover this insight:

- It takes time to understand your own dust cloud.
- You can't use someone else's dust as your excuse for not achieving your goal.
- Just because you can identify someone else's dust doesn't make it good.
- Wishing and hoping are not courses of action.
- Every choice you've made up to now has created your present life; your future life will depend on the choice you make in the next fifteen minutes.

- You are in control only of your response to your environment.
- Emotional tornados are a combination of wind and dust, and they are never worth the thrill of the ride.

The memories we drag with us through life, like Linus and his blanket, are there because we choose to hold onto them. When people undertake spring cleaning and suddenly come across a telephone number of someone nice they once met, or a box containing the baby teeth of their child, they experience a spurt of emotion from a newly ignited memory. The emotional charge may be positive or negative, depending upon the memories activated. These "trigger objects" rekindle memories in the same way a tone of voice can create an emotional undertow, calling up misplaced anger or fear related to a time long ago. All too often this internal alarm spurs us to respond inappropriately to the person or situation in the present. These moments can throw us and those around us into chaos, if we don't remember to stay in the present. They can take us from planned to snap decision-making in a nanosecond and can jeopardize our ability to get to our goal. In their wake, we usually find regret, anger, and exhaustion.

HOW TO AVOID GETTING SWEPT OUT IN AN EMOTIONAL UNDERTOW

Daniel Goldman, noted author on emotional intelligence, discusses the impact of memory on the psyche and day-to-day survival in his 2003 book, *Emotional Intelligence*. Memory, as an evolutionary survival tool, allows animals and humans to improve decision-making and increase the potential for survival. The memory of getting sick from eating a certain plant would teach one to avoid the plant in the future. Goldman explains, however, that "memory is state specific."[7] In other words, depending upon our state of mind, we color in our memory of an event. If we're happy at the time we're focusing our attention on an event, then we remember the positive things. On the other hand, if we're unhappy, we use a negative filter to capture all the aspects that we notice as unfavorable.

YOUR CENTER OF THE UNIVERSE

Each of us remembers things from our distinct, individual, and private center of the universe. We experience our life events, editing the real and the reel through the lens of emotion and past experience. If you find that your memories change over time, it's normal. Humans are not able to report exact occurrences without the vulnerability of altering perspectives. This is why, when gathering information from eyewitnesses at the scene of an accident, investigators use multiple, separate accounts to paint an overall picture. The bias we place on an event is reflected in what we notice, what we decide to remember, and what we choose to forget. "Memory is attention in the past tense: what you remember now is what you noticed before."[8]

Our consciousness might forget a painful memory in an attempt to soothe our traumatized psyche. Goldman tells us that "memory is autobiography: its author is the 'self.'"[9] Your "self" is comprised of multiple patterns of thinking and behaving. The self acts as a newscaster, censoring, deleting, and editing the information that forms our memories.[10] As with the weather, we are usually aware of our emotional state only when it is exceptionally good or bad. On most other days, we are more concerned with our to-do list. Our private emotional climate is either a hindrance or an added benefit toward accomplishing our goals.

Most of us really tune into our emotions only when they are high or low; otherwise, we virtually ignore them. However, just because the outside temperature is not freezing or burning the sweat off our skin, doesn't mean that the atmosphere is not affecting our physical cooling system. When we're comfortable, we don't pay close attention to weather conditions *or* our emotions. We go on emotional autopilot and turn down our self-awareness. But if you want to be happy and become who you could have been, this is a mistake! So here are two important words for the day, week, month, year, and lifetime: *pay attention!*

TURN UP THE VOLUME OF SELF-AWARENESS

Athletes are highly aware of the outside temperature. Ironman competitors always consider the outside temperature, humidity, and elevation of the environments they train and compete in. They develop an acute ability to interpret subtle atmospheric changes, as well as anticipate alterations in their physical environment. These athletes appreciate the enormous price their bodies will have to pay to correct any added stress that might ensue. The preparation involved in successfully training for an Ironman competition is a perfect example of self-determined, positive-outcome decision-making. Ironman competitors pay close attention, not only when it matters, but all the time—because in the long run, it does matter all the time. They watch existing patterns and usual events, and then they consider what effect these will have on the body's ability to perform.

The climate they *can* exert control over—their own bodies—they do control, and they prepare for the climate that they can't control. To achieve what Goldman would consider emotionally intelligent decision-making, we need to adopt this perspective. We need to control the climate we can control, which is our response to our environment, and prepare for the environment we cannot control, which refers to other people and their emotional environments. So how does this play out with your dust storm? Each person needs to be aware of his or her own emotional dust, and begin the cleanup. Some of the greatest problems we encounter arise when we choose to believe that we have the ability to control others.

Implementing Marshall's Law #6 (you are only in control of your response to your environment) requires some skills to back it up. It is important, however, that you give up the ridiculous thought that you somehow have the ability to control others. You're just wasting your precious time and finite energy. You can't control them—hey, you can't even control yourself sometimes!

It's time for you to choose to move to a position of strength. Refocus your attention on what can, or will, make you happy. Begin by evaluating your immediate emotional environment the way professional athletes evaluate their physical environments. Consciously put yourself on a course that leads to your goal. This awareness of emotional environments brings us back to the Pig Pen Theory of Immediate Emotional Environments.

IMMEDIATE EMOTIONAL ENVIRONMENTS (IE2)

Consider an airplane full of people listening to their choice of music or videos through headphones. Now imagine that everyone suddenly takes their headphones off and broadcasts their private entertainment to the public universe. The cacophony would be deafening. Each person's IE2 is a compilation of noisy, individualized, emotionally laden memory "dust." To become the you that you could have been involves creating and supporting a positive IE2. This process uses self-awareness and self-direction as filters because the emotional playlist that makes up your IE2 is not comprised of random memories. Each person has memories that are chosen, ones that are cultivated, and ones that have buried themselves in our souls without our knowledge or permission.

Armed with the knowledge that we have no control over anyone or anything except for our response to our environment, it's time to work on our emotional hygiene, decrease the emotional noise, and dampen the memory dust. We accomplish this when we apply our energy to maintaining a daily positive IE2. How can you do this? Increase your self- awareness, and tune in to the emotional environments of those around you. You have the ability to choose which emotional environments you want to travel in and to purposefully engage in strategies to minimize, deflect, or avoid the negative IE2s of others.

CHOOSING POSITIVE IE2S

How can you identify people with positive IE2s? Typically, these people are optimistic and fun to be around. They're not bossy, and they don't complain or blame others for their failures.

Have you ever seen children spinning around and around with their arms outstretched and their eyes closed? They play out this ritual dance in public and private, with or without adults watching. They don't stop spinning until they are totally dizzy. They usually do it more than once, even though after the first time they know they might fall down, feel sick to their stomachs, and maybe even throw up. This spinning ritual is a common childhood behavior. Most of the time this kind of thrill-seeking behavior loses its appeal after one or two bad tumbles, a bruised head, or a hurt ego. The danger surfaces, however, when the draw of the thrill is due to the possibility of personal injury rather than the novelty of a new experience. People who are attracted to and excited by the near-miss experiences in childhood and adolescence often move from physical spinning to manipulative emotional spinning when they grow up. They become virtual tornadoes of emotion, with little to no self-determined behavior skills and even less concern about the collateral damage they inflict on those around them. They will sweep in anyone who gets close enough to their swirling, emotionally charged dust cloud, sucking innocent bystanders into their current drama and leaving them behind in the wake of the storm.

Tornado by Proxy

Mark was easygoing. He had his strange little habits, like having to make his own espresso every morning in an old percolator his grandfather left him, but for the most part he chugged through his days without any major drama. Most days he would go to work and enjoy his day. Suddenly, though, all this changed.

Mark consistently began to have bad mornings at work. He would get to work angry and by lunchtime would have experienced at least one argument. He realized that his friend Mindy, who had recently moved to his city, had begun to call each morning, engrossing him in the trials of her daily experiences. Her dramatic stories would get him so involved in the lives of people he didn't even know that he was an emotional tornado by the time he got to work.

Soon he realized that a call from Mindy, who had been his friend a long time, was all he needed to ruin his morning. He began to screen his calls until he could meet with her and set up some boundaries related to their conversations. Not long after he stopped listening to Mindy's tirades, his days went back to normal.

Mindy and Mark represent extremes, with Mindy explosive to the point of infective, and Mark's compromised emotional immunity dangerously low. Most of us lie somewhere in the middle of these two extremes, sometimes getting swept into other people's problems and dramas but also being able to enjoy long periods of emotional balance. The skill is to identify your own IE2, be aware of the IE2s of those around you, and prepare for eventual mixing of the "dust clouds." The key is to mindfully choose action over either reaction or inaction. The degree of difficulty a person experiences in this decision-making process is directly related to his or her capacity to identify a goal. When you know what you want to have happen next, then you can choose the behavior that is most likely going to make it happen.

SUMMARY

Immediate Emotional Environments (IE2) are comprised of our emotionally charged memories as well as those of the people around us. Getting some insight into our own IE2 can help us disengage those behaviors that are triggered by our memories, not our present situations, and do not help us move forward in our lives. When we choose to turn up the volume of our self-awareness, we can predict with more certainty what we need to do to achieve our goals. Focusing on positive outcomes, the actions that will bring us there, and the people who support us in our quest helps us make what we want to have happen next a reality.

CHAPTER 13

EMOTIONALLY BASED BEHAVIORS

Behavior is action that is visible, measurable, and identifiable. When we have goals and we can identify what we want to have happen next, we are able to base our behavior on the likely outcome of an action. Our acting logic is "If I do this, that will happen." It is usually the *why* of what we choose to do. When we base our behavior upon a reaction to an immediate threat or an intense emotional experience, then it is an emotionally based behavior. These behaviors respond to the immediate emotional environment (IE2), not to your mindful purpose. When people lose sight of who they wanted to become, it is very often due to multiple, emotionally based behavioral responses. It's akin to putting fires out in the immediate environment without planning for installing a sprinkler system. We find this kind of response especially attractive when we're faced with overwhelming change, such as experiencing a traumatic event that results in the loss of a home, job, or life.

Fighting Change with Hyper-Change

Bea lost her mother and father during the same year, only weeks apart. One died of cancer, the other of a heart attack. In a very short time, Bea lost all that was familiar to her, as well as her faith in the future.

"I am suspended in the horror of death—in an endless black hole," she would say. "I don't want to ever love again. Comfort in the familiar is the devil, so I will never allow someone to get that close to me again. After all, the person is just going to die and leave me."

Bea quit her job and began to travel extensively. Soon she took a new job that required three weeks of traveling a month. Upon returning home, she would recount stories of people she met and speak about plans to reconnect with them. She intuitively minimized her loss by planning her changes and stockpiling memories and events that satisfied the suction of the vacuum.

Three years later she entered a committed relationship, settled down, and started a family of her own.

When Bea first ran away, she thought that eliminating the "stuff" would eradicate the feeling of loss or the need to refill it. The vacuum, however, isn't about stuff, even though stuff sometimes gets sucked into it; the vacuum is really about comfort. All change, no matter how small, disturbs the balance of our comfort. Usually the disturbance is small enough that it doesn't cause any real problems, but sometimes it starts a chain of events that leads to more loss, more vacuums, and more loss of comfort than we bargained for. Soon we find ourselves standing next to the crater carved by our temper tantrum, and we wonder how things ever got so out of hand.

RUNNING AWAY FROM CHANGE

A typical emotional response to tragic events is to run away. The child in each of us wants to get away from the problem. The adult part of the personality, however, will step into the decision-making process to remind us that the consequences of today's decisions might surrender our future to choices we don't want to have to make. This kind of decision-making often occurs during divorce proceedings, when each partner is so angry with the other that they cannot make logical choices. So lawyers step in to remind us how today's decision might impact the future. Emotionally based behaviors are also at the heart of great romance and literature. Romeo and Juliet, for example, demonstrate how young people who have fallen in love and can't imagine a day away from each other are consumed by their relationship and will even consider suicide before solitude. Decisions made during periods of extreme emotional turmoil rarely provide a positive outcome.

EMOTIONAL RESPONSE TO EXTREME CHANGE

Do you remember ever hearing news that really threw you for a loop? The experience can be cataclysmic. The sensation of loss and the feeling you get when you answer the phone and someone tells you news that you did not want to hear has been described in multiple ways.

- The Earth opens up and swallows me whole.
- There is a great noise in my head, and although people around me are talking, I can see only the movement of their lips, rather than hearing their voices.
- There is only deafening silence. I find myself staring at men's ties or women's jewelry.

When tragic events engulf us, our human nature protects us. It automatically begins to shield us from the sense of unbearable loss. Despite living through loss and emotional pain, we search for reasons, causes, ways to deny what is real, and ways to comfort ourselves.

Some things you already know:

- All change is loss.
- Loss creates vacuums.
- Vacuums are unstable and can precipitate emotional upheavals.
- Experiencing an emotional upheaval can lead to the fear of being consumed by the sense of loss.

PREDICTING EXTREME RESPONSES

Tragic experiences produce a predictable emotional reaction, a passage through multiple stages—denial, anger, bargaining, depression, and acceptance—that Dr. Elizabeth Kubler-Ross has identified as the stages of death and dying.[11] We can apply these stages to something as simple as getting into the car and finding out that it won't start, as I've done here.

1. **DENIAL.** What's the first thing you do? You try to start it again! And again. You may check to make sure the radio, heater, lights, and so on are off. Then you try again.

2. **ANGER.** "%$@^##& car! I should have junked you years ago." Do you slam your hand on the steering wheel? I have. "I should just leave you out in the rain and let you rust."

3. **BARGAINING.** Realizing that you're going to be late for work: "Oh please, car, if you will just start one more time I promise I'll buy you a brand-new battery, get a tune-up and new tires and belts and hoses. I'll keep you in perfect working condition."

4. **DEPRESSION.** "Oh, God, what am I going to do? I'm going to be late for work. I give up. My job is at risk, and I don't really care anymore. What's the use?"

5. **ACCEPTANCE.** "Okay, it's dead. Guess I'd better call the Auto Club or find another way to work. Time to get on with my day; I'll deal with this later."

Years of research and scientific documentation has demonstrated the predictability of these reactions. We know these stages as they apply to death and dying, but Kubler-Ross first outlined them as the five stages of receiving catastrophic news. I find that this description describes the broader scope and definition of loss.

All change is loss, and when the specific loss experience is perceived to be catastrophic, then the five stages of loss would occur. We can expect these reactions after any personally important event, from the moving of furniture to the loss of a loved one. We experience the five stages as an instinctual human reaction to perceived loss.

When the expectation of an event occurring and the reality of that loss collide, an emotional vacuum occurs. Vacuums are unstable, frightening places—voids that require filling. When an emotional void is created, human beings instinctually protect their emotional well-being by passing through the multiple stages of grief, which can lead them back to a perceived state of emotional equilibrium. According to Dr. Kubler- Ross, that journey ends in the acceptance of what is.

These predictable, normal stages of grief represent our instinctual, emotionally based reaction to loss. At the same time, we can use these emotional responses to excuse behaviors that we choose to exhibit, or we can use them to allow ourselves to spin out of control in an emotional tornado. Knowing about these stages can make us comfortable excusing overt acts of anger, denial, depression, and the occasional bargaining, such as hearing a friend say, "I promise I won't smoke anymore if I, or the person I love, can just beat this cancer for a year." Just like the divorcee or Romeo and Juliet, when a friend begins to make emotionally based decisions during catastrophic events, someone needs to be the voice of reason.

BEWARE OF THE MOUSETRAPS!

We must learn to avoid a major mousetrap, or behavior trap, when we are faced with emotionally based behaviors. The immediate emotional environment surrounding a person gripped by loss is highly unstable. When we identify that the person is in the stages of loss and we accept the behaviors as a part of his or her rite of passage in dealing with the loss, we can unthinkingly begin to tolerate the person's "dust cloud" at abnormally high levels for extended periods of time. We normalize the abnormal behaviors! We often base our response to the person on a choice that comforts *us*, rather than one that helps the person with the loss move toward a healthy goal. We, in effect, enter into the person's altered emotional reality. By going along with the emotionally based behaviors, we are choosing to deny what we know is right, and we might actually be deceiving ourselves into believing that we can change things back to the way they were. In other words, we enter into the person's emotional delusion, denying reality and insight for short-lived emotional comfort.

The reality of "the way it was" reflects a composite memory based on our focus in the past. The stories we hear from our parents, or that we ourselves tell, paint a rosy picture of childhood and innocence that denies the more difficult experiences. Oftentimes that reality is a pipe dream and has nothing to do with what we need in our present to get to our future. Emotional memories of *how things were* can present a distorted, sculpted view of our past; we should not rely on them as reliable maps for making future choices. Usually we choose to keep things as they were because we desire the familiar, not because they relate to what we want to have happen next. I have never been one to accept something as right or good just because that's how it usually happens. Life is too short not to pursue your goals!

> **MARSHALL'S LAW #8: Accepting things because "that's the way things are" produces a false sense of comfort.** To become accustomed to, accept, and support behaviors only because they occur in a predictable, repeating pattern is a recipe for disaster.

ALTERNATIVE CHOICES OF DOING NOTHING

Understanding behaviors that accompany learned helplessness reminds us that when we think it's normal to have no control over the future, we just stop trying to make things better. In those moments, we resign ourselves to "this is the way it is" thinking. We give power to habitual decision-making, and in the process, reinforce our own negative circumstances. In short, we succumb to the vacuum.

Break free from learned helplessness by implementing strategies and skills that open you to identifying alternative choices. The more choices you are able to identify, the more likely you will find one or two that will be beneficial and ultimately return you to decision-making and actions that lead to your desired outcomes.

BELIEVING IN CHOICE

So how do people learn to believe that they really have choices? They learn through making choices—little ones that succeed. Instead of habitually submitting to our vacuums and undermining alibis, we need to develop empowering, self-determined strategies that enable us to crawl out of our foxholes of helplessness and begin moving in the direction of our real, self-determined happiness.

MARSHALL'S LAW #9: You cannot expect anyone else to save you. Hoping and wishing are not action verbs, nor are they reliable plans of action to get out of the vacuum of loss. Each person must develop skills to save him or herself. **Waiting to be rescued will no longer be accepted as a valid strategic plan of action.**

Knowing about the stages of loss provides us with support and guidance during hard times, the same way belief buffers help us get through emotionally trying situations. As with belief buffers, do not use any of the stages as a long-term strategy to cope with loss. When a person stalls in one of the stages of loss for any prolonged period of time, he or she injures and sometimes destroys the life that remains. When you or someone you know has made that stall a chronic method of coping, it may be time to seek professional guidance.

The five stages of receiving catastrophic news represent an automatic reaction to the external circumstances of our lives—circumstances that are not within our control. The only thing we *can* control is how we choose to respond to our circumstances.

Emotionally based behaviors, despite their volatility, are usually predictable, which is why we can categorize them into stages. Choosing to continue to your goal, despite the temptations to slide back into your comfortable old ways, engages you in the process of active outcome planning. Once you have learned how to enjoy the process, the outcome ceases to be the goal; it becomes the predictable eventuality.

So how can a person avoid the mousetraps of temptation? How can you defend yourself from sliding back into old reactive behaviors? Some effective tools exist for this use. Do you know what kinds of tools you should have on hand to keep yourself from getting sucked into the vacuum? A good start is to identify the kinds of habitual choices you make that produce unwanted behaviors and outcomes. Usually these are habits you don't think about, but you engage in them every day. If your habitual behaviors trigger negative emotional responses from the people you work/live/play with, you are probably undermining your ability to get the outcomes you desire.

Emotions are like watches; they look like simple timepieces, but below the face they are very complicated. To avoid the multiple emotional mousetraps that can derail your best intentions on the way to becoming you, analyze what is and isn't working in your present routine. Then, determine how you can positively change to help reach your goal. There are some specific tools that will be described in Chapter 15 that will be able to help you cut through, or eliminate, the behaviors that are preventing you from achieving your goals.

SUMMARY

Emotionally based behaviors are often automatic responses to implicit memories. They may arise from one of the five stages of grief that has caught us and kept us from moving toward a better life. Getting lulled into complacency by thoughts that enforce the status quo, or demanding that someone else fix your life, will only keep you frozen in time. Gaining happiness is a choice that you must make. Depending how long you have been trapped in old behaviors, the victim role might appear to be more comfortable. However, engaging in new behaviors and taking small steps will help you break free of the bonds of the mousetraps caused by your tired, old, ineffective, out-dated belief busters.

CHAPTER 14

MOUSETRAPS AND EMOTIONAL SPINS

It, They, or I?	
Some will say *it*:	"The universe is at fault."
Others will say *they*:	"The situation/other people are at fault."
Still others will say *I*:	"I made the choice. How could I have done this differently?"
Which viewpoint fits your style?	

How you define your situation directly impacts the size of your vacuum. It also will determine your ability to identify working strategies that will guide you first to a place of personal comfort and then eventually to happiness. For some people, life has a slow leak when it comes to their happiness. The subtle, day-to-day assaults on people's goals and dreams have blinded them to what they have lost along the way. They feel that retrieving or re-creating the dream is an impossible task, and they resign themselves to accepting things as they are. Suddenly, the energy required for implementing change exits by some invisible back door, and silent permission is given to sink back into the comfy couch of unmet and expired expectations.

Wake up!

Choosing to own your goal also demands ownership of actions and outcomes! We live in a world of immediate gratification. The process of achieving a goal often seems like a tedious experience—one to engage in only as a necessary evil to reach the prize.

As long as the process is the enemy, the goal will be in jeopardy!

Mousetraps are set with cheese because that's what mice are looking for. Mousetraps work because they make mice think that there's an easy way to get food. The mouse is tempted to give up looking for a meal and instead steal the piece of cheese that is just sitting there, waiting to be taken. Next thing you know, *slam!* No more dinner, no more mouse!

What are some of the inherent mousetraps that people experience on the way to becoming who they could have been? The following negative personal characteristics that I like to call barrier personalities increase the likelihood of getting caught in mousetraps. Barrier personalities have a built-in, wireless communication for failure. It is a well-known fact that the mouse that has eaten a fine meal will not be tempted by the bait; only the mouse that's on a food quest will even stop to smell the cheese.

FOUR BARRIER PERSONALITIES

THE PROCRASTINATOR

Procrastinators typically talk about the great importance of making the change, and they finds loads of methods to help with the change. In fact, procrastinators spend so much time looking for methods to change that they have little time left to implement any one method. By the time they have identified a goal, it's time to go to sleep or take a vacation or buy a new car. The behavior required to reach the goal is postponed until another day.

Key words: "Just a minute"; "I'm so busy right now—maybe tomorrow"; "Don't worry, we have plenty of time and I've got a number of different ways to get it done"; "No problem—I still have another day to get it all done."

THE DENIER

The denier doesn't have a problem; it's only a temporary difficulty that will self-resolve. Besides, it's not that bad, and even if it were, it's only bad because that's the way other people make it seem. Really, there's no problem, so there's no need for a solution.

Key words: "Me, worry?"; "What's the matter? I don't see any problem"; "Why do you always have to make a big deal of everything? You'll see— nothing's going to happen because everything is okay the way it is."

THE QUITTER

Quitters never even give themselves a chance to reach their goals. Quitters usually lack the motivation for change or assign little or no value to achieving the change. Oftentimes quitting is the first symptom of learned helplessness. After all, if it doesn't make any difference whether you act, why not just quit? The quitter has no self-confidence and no desire to reach the goal.

Key words: "I quit"; "*Fine*"; "I'm out of here!"

THE BLAMER

It is never the blamer's fault. These are the people whose dogs ate their homework, who never got fair chances in life, and who will somehow implicate everyone around them as the cause of their misery. According to the blamer, if you hadn't walked in when you did, the blamer would have been able to do whatever it was that was expected.

Key words: "It's all *your* fault"; "If *you* hadn't … "; "because of *you*, I … "; "Why do *you* always have to …"

Whether or not you can identify yourself in one of these four personalities, you likely can identify others in them. If your barrier friends bring their emotional dust into your plans, it's easy to fall into their mousetraps. All these personalities have two things in common: none of them are responsible for their outcomes, and all of them are experts at being emotional spin doctors. A person who has the ability to color a fact in a way that changes the real meaning, thereby altering the listener's reaction, is a "spin doctor."

IDENTIFYING YOUR EMOTIONAL SPIN

What is emotional spin? Emotional spin is the poignant bias that we put onto actions that are inconsistent to achieving a result. We miss the bus, and we cry about how ill we felt that morning. We don't want to go to a gathering, so we talk about how badly we are treated in the presence of the person we want to avoid. It is a manipulation of the situation and an attempt to destablize the emotional environment to create an illusion of support and to justify behaviors we know will turn out badly. In the following story, Jennifer's emotional spin drags up anger and feelings of victimization in an attempt to make her impulsive purchase more acceptable.

Solo Spinning

Jennifer wanted to buy herself a pair of earrings. She knew that it was an extravagant expenditure, but times had been bad and she really wanted a specific pair.

She anticipated her partner's negative response, played out the scenario, got very angry at her partner's anticipated response, bought the earrings from the joint account anyway, and went home. When she walked into the house, she openly and defiantly announced, "I don't care if you think it was a good idea—I bought the earrings anyway!"

Her partner's response was one of confused insult, and an argument quickly ensued.

Solo spinning is very dangerous. It demands that the spinner engages in creating an active, willful, and malicious emotional tornado with the sole intention of covering up negative behaviors. Quite often this method of displacing personal responsibility for bad decision-making begins in childhood. The more successful it is, the more it will be employed. In children it usually takes the form of tantrums; with adults, however, it can result in explosive outrage, creating emotional disasters that have long-term effects on all who experience them.

If you are like the solo spinner, you might interpret the world around you as hostile, and you need to fight to get what you want. It may be difficult to see that you are creating the future that you fearfully anticipate. Interpreting the events from the center of our own individual universe limits our perspective and our ability to see multiple possible choices and outcomes.

We can try to see through the eyes of others, but invariably we interpret the environment and the people in it through our own personalized set of glasses. This is why understanding our personal brand of spinning is so important. When our experiences are good, we look to attribute our success to something we did or something in the environment that acted in our favor. If we feel that we've failed, we color the experience with this same paintbrush. Regardless of the outcome, it is our belief that a causal relationship exists between the environment, our behavior, and consequences that serves as a guideline for our future behavior in similar situations. Gathering information about past experiences, and sharing expectations with others, can help reduce the need for personal spinning and unexpected negative outcomes.

Same Rally Different Memories

Zoe and Sean went to a rally for a political figure. Zoe knew all about the rally and dragged Sean along, promising a great evening of interesting conversation and good food. When Zoe met Sean at the door, she noticed that Sean had dressed very casually, whereas most of the other attendants were in business clothes.

The two talked to a number of candidates, mingled with the volunteers, and ate a delicious self-serve dinner. Around 10 PM, Sean, who had been one of the more animated attendants and had actively worked the room, thanked Zoe for the invite and went home.

Three weeks later, Zoe and Sean were talking with KC, who invited them to a lecture by one of the candidates. Sean looked down and stated flatly, "I really don't enjoy these political get-togethers. It's not about the issues—it's just about being seen." Zoe was shocked, having thought that Sean had really enjoyed his experience at the rally.

ATTRIBUTION THEORY

If you think that something you do will result in a specific outcome, you are more likely to engage in that behavior when you want that outcome. Human beings need to explain *why* things happen. We want to understand our world and be able to affect it in a way that will produce dependable, expected results. A perfect example is hailing a cab. If you think that standing in the street and waving your arm will cause a cab to stop for you, you are likely to do this movement when you look to hail a cab; if you don't have this belief, chances are you won't engage in the behavior. Fritz Heidler first presented this theory in 1958, and psychologists, theorists, and behaviorists have embraced it ever since.[12, 13] When you believe that an action you take will result in a specific, desired outcome, you are more likely to engage in that action. Think back to the *It, They, I* discussion. To what do you attribute your successes and failures? Are they due to fate/the universe, other people, or yourself?

Attribution Theory and Hailing a Cab

Tim and Terry walked out of their Upper East Side apartment on a rainy afternoon. Tim looked up and down York Avenue and then handed Terri the umbrella. "Why are you giving me this?" she asked.

"Because it's raining and I never have luck when it's raining. You, on the other hand, have taxi mojo!"

"I have long arms and a loud whistle—that's all" she responded.

She took the umbrella, stretched out her left arm, and put her right hand to her mouth. Seconds later she let out a loud whistle. A taxi pulled over, and Tim and Terry were on their way to the restaurant.

INTENTION, CONTROL, AND BEHAVIOR

The level of control you that believe you have over achieving a desired goal will determine whether you engage in the action to get there.[14] If you think you have no control over the outcome, then it doesn't matter what you do—the outcome is out of your control. A good example of this kind of thinking is when a person says, "I'm going to die anyway, so why not smoke?" However, if you believe that your actions will impact the outcome, your behavior will change to exert control toward your desired goal. "If I stop smoking today, I'll improve my health and I'll be alive and dancing at my daughter's wedding."

Changing Behavior and Believing in Your Outcome

On the street corner at Mim's house is a crosswalk with a button for pedestrians. When Mim wants to cross the street, a push of the button changes the light. Every day Mim pushes the button because she believes that the action causes the light to change. Tyra, Mim's partner, gives a sigh and shakes her head when Mim pushes the button.

"What's the matter now? Mim asks.

"You! Why do you waste your time pushing that button? It doesn't do anything!" replies Tyra.

"Have you ever tried?" Mim asks.

"I don't waste my time. Everyone knows it's just a ploy to make you feel as though you have some control!" Tyra steps into the street.

Seconds later the light changes and Mim walks to catch up with Tyra.

In situations where you believe that the locus of control is in your power, you are motivated to act. When you feel that there is no connection between your action and the outcome, and that no matter what action you take, the outcome will remain the same, you are not motivated to act. Just like Tyra and Mim, deciding to push the button at the crosswalk is an easy change to make once you have determined that your action actually changes the light. The simple choice allows you to get to the other side more quickly, and reduces the risk of being hit by an oncoming car. What about the changes that require us to give up a habit or an addiction? How can we program ourselves to sustain a change in behavior that removes an action that we've incorporated fully into our lives? Like Margo and Savannah in the following example, the reasons we choose to change must fit our own lives and priorities.

Natural Change and Proactive Change

When Savannah moved into her fifth-floor, walk-up apartment in Chicago, she was a light smoker. She thought that smoking was cool and that it helped her keep her weight down. Once she moved into her apartment, however, she found that she was out of breath by the time she reached the third floor. This feeling of breathlessness annoyed her, and her enjoyment of smoking was diminished by the experience. Savannah soon stopped buying and smoking cigarettes.

Margo quit smoking two years earlier when she realized the effect that smoking would have on her unborn child. She knew it would be difficult to stop, so she called up her local smoking cessation program and began classes.

Savannah's decision to give up cigarettes reflected the realization that the annoyances that came with her smoking habit outweighed her perceived benefits of smoking. She decided that either she had to find a new place to live or give up smoking. Quitting smoking was the easier, more natural choice.

Margo's decision, however, was not a natural choice, but a proactive change. She decided that the habit/addiction would be bad for her future and the future of her child, so she changed the behavior with the help of professionals. Margo's smoking did not have the annoying, constant negative impact on her life that Savannah's did, but Margo realized that to get to her long-term goal of a healthy child, she had to eliminate her behavior of smoking.

When you think about your home-base behavior, are you looking to change it because it is interfering with your short-term happiness, or is it because it will be the undoing of a long-term goal? It's important to clearly define this difference; sometimes the changes we make to achieve short-term, transient happiness can be positive, as was the case with Savannah. Other times however, focusing on short-term highs can derail long term plans. A person who wants to end a long and rewarding relationship or job to pursue the thrill of a riskier or more exciting one might achieve the change with some difficulty but find that, in the long term, the vacuum it creates can never be successfully filled again.

When choosing a proactive behavior change, set concrete short-term goals that you can accomplish. "Touching the Void" is a powerful film that clearly demonstrates the power of short-term, self-determined behavior. The film introduces us to two young mountain climbers and portrays how each was able to face the challenge of seemingly insurmountable odds. How these men clarified their immediate problems, refocused on solutions, and never entertained the belief that their own locus of control was determined by anyone other than themselves, sheds light into the heart of self-determined behavior.

MARSHALL'S LAW #10: **All change is loss.** Plan for it, and understand that loss of any kind will produce a vacuum. All vacuums are unstable and seek to be stabilized. Before you change a behavior, learn your replacement behavior.

By choosing to change a behavior, we are in fact choosing to give up a piece of comfort. When we decide that our future is a direct result of the choices we make on a daily basis, and that each loss we incur on the way to our goal is a positive one, we begin to be responsible for our choices. The greatest loss we can suffer is the loss of our dreams and hopes for tomorrow. These losses usually result not from change, but from our inability to change and adjust during the voyage. To choose self-determination is to lose your excuses and ready yourself for solving the challenge of tomorrow.

SUMMARY

Your choice of defining your environment and your ability to effect positive change in it will impact your capacity to engage in positive outcome decision-making. Supporting your successes with fact, rather than solo spinning around your disappointments, paves the road to success. Know the outcome you want to achieve, identify your actions and intentions, and engage in the behavior that keeps the power of what happens next to you in your hands.

CHAPTER 15

THE TOOLBOX

Bernard Baruch, a famous businessman and presidential advisor, once said, "When all you have in your toolbox is a hammer, everything starts looking like a nail." Emotions are like china vases, so it's time to put the hammers away and add more effective tools to your repertoire.

When you are really angry and want to yell, scream, or haul off and hit someone, you're using the hammer. In any playground, you can overhear adults telling angry and frustrated children, "Use your words." The adult soothes the child back to rational thought and helps him or her regain stability, but what happens to adults in similar situations? Who is there to remind *us* to use our words, to plan our actions, to think before we act when an emotional tornado overtakes us? Usually it's the people who know that it's not impossible to get the results you want. They understand that to achieve happiness on the way to attaining a goal requires patience, flexibility, and planning.

When caught in the winds of emotional tornadoes, mistakes are made, words are used as weapons, and attitudes turn hot and cold. Knowing where and when you are likely to need shelter, a guiding light, or a quick excuse can make even the worst disaster less threatening. Having a toolbox that has strategies and methods to protect you from the oncoming adversity can provide you with positive outcome options in a time of high emotional stress. In Chapter 13, you were promised a toolbox that would provide you with ways to avoid decision-making during emotionally unstable times. To start off, you will have five tools in your toolbox. These are general tools that you can employ in a variety of situations. As you become more skilled with these tools, you will be able to identify other tools that will heighten the precision and accuracy of this basic set.

MARSHALL'S LAW #11: It is the craftsperson, not the tool, that brings success. The tools in your toolbox are only as effective as the person who uses them. A tool used incorrectly or on the wrong job will not successfully achieve the desired goal. The more practice the user has, the better the tool performs.

IDENTIFYING EXISTING TOOLS

Before getting to the tools, it's helpful to identify potential problems or situations that will require you to adjust your behavior. Most of the tools we have in adulthood are either inherited from our families or picked up from observing others. A cautionary word: many of the tools you've been lugging around don't work anymore; they are antiquated, or even worse, obsolete. Many of these tools worked only in your home, and when you tried to import them into other situations, you immediately saw their worthlessness. However, giving them up meant creating a vacuum. Without something to replace them with, they cropped up again and again, never solving the problem but always at hand to be used in a pinch.

TOOLS TO TRASH

1. *Repeating our parent's mistakes.* Have you every thought to yourself, "Oh gosh—I'm sounding like my parents!" If you haven't, you are in the minority. Many of us grew up in homes where we heard threats like "Your wait till your father gets home," bullying comments like "You do as I say because it's my house," or parental masochism like "This hurts me more than it does you." If these statements were the tools of your caregivers, then your coat of armor is a pair of work pants and your hammer is probably on a bungee cord attached to your hip! Of course, each time you use that hammer, it ricochets back into your pocket and causes an emotional black-and-blue spot that, though persistently tender, you expect to hit on every emotionally charged day. After all, you know it's going to happen. The strange part is that, like it or not, when it hits the sensation is strangely both comforting and limiting.

All I can say is *cut the cord*. Get rid of the hammer and its bungee cord. It's hurting you. If it helps, tell yourself that your parents, or whoever used it on you, didn't know any better. After all, they were the duck-and-cover believers! They didn't have the kinds of tools available to them that you have. Cut the cord, empty the box, and start from scratch. You'll be happy to know that I've described most of the ineffective tools (like emotional spinning and barrier personality behaviors) in one fashion or another in all the pages up to now, so replacing them should not cause too much of a vacuum.

When we grow up watching our parents and their parents deal with life, we are learning their tools. Over time the situations and needs change, but too often the tools do not.

Changing Tools Over Time

1958   9:30 AM Drew is watching the black-and-white TV flicker with gyrating bodies of teens moving to music on *American Bandstand*. Wavy lines disrupt the picture, and Drew gets up and hits the side of the television with a quick punch. The lines disappear.

1968   9 PM Drew is watching *The Ed Sullivan Show* in color. Little white dots (called snow) interfere with the picture. Pat, his child, swiftly kicks the TV and the picture seems to improve.

5 PM Drew is listening to a new-fangled music box called a Walkman. The tape cassette is sounding a little funny, so he hits it and shakes it. Nothing happens. His grandchild KC takes the Walkman. "It's not broken, Pop-Pop. Watch … "Gently KC opens the back, replaces the batteries, and then hands it back to Drew, who skeptically puts on the headphones. "Changing the batteries is a good idea, but this is the magic that makes it work," Drew says as he taps the little box a few times, turns it on, and listens to the music. "Listen to Pop-Pop. He knows how to make things work," says Pat. They exchange knowing looks, and all of them smile.

5 AM KC's Blackberry rings. "Hello? Hello?" The irritation in his drowsy voice is palpable. "Hello?" KC repeats in aggravation. He strains to make out the caller ID, sees that it's home, and gets worried. Sitting up suddenly, KC reaches over and taps the Blackberry on the bedside table. It breaks in half and goes dead. "Great magic," KC groans.

GETTING EXPERT ADVICE

Once you realize that you should allow people who know what they're doing to repair your appliances, life gets so much easier! Suddenly you won't be angry at the TV, radio, toaster, or microwave for not living up to your expectations. You will be able to take responsibility for making sure that their malfunctioning will not be the variable that impacts your day.

How many times has your day started off badly because your alarm, which often shuts off, didn't get you out of bed on time? What about the car that constantly overheats in the summer, so that you drive with the heat on to cool the engine? By the time you get to your destination, you're soaked with perspiration and angry enough to want to just go home. All too often we allow ourselves to be manipulated into a bad mood by our gadgets, machinery, and other "helpful" devices that malfunction on a regular basis! It's time to take stock of the mechanical and physical clutter that is polluting our emotional environments.

If your mantra is "I don't have money to repair it," then at least accept the fact that choosing to use a malfunctioning appliance can cost you more than money. Of course, you should apply "if it ain't broke, don't fix it" to both your physical and emotional worlds. Here are some simple steps to take in the material world to eliminate dysfunction:

- When the television stops working, first see if the plug is in before hitting it, or worse yet, taking it apart.
- If you know that your elevator is slow and jerky, and you steel yourself each time you use it, choose to take the stairs.
- Choose to toss the leaky, plastic coffee container (yeah, the one you've had since college), and wake up early enough to sit down and have a cup of joe or tea at your kitchen table like a human being.

CHOOSING YOUR RESPONSE

Steps you might need to take in the emotional/well-being aspect of your life are not as clear-cut. The most important rule to remember is that no matter what the situation is, *you only have control over how you choose to respond*—nothing else. If you choose to give up your control over how you respond, you have essentially given the keys to your emotional kingdom to the very person who is actively pushing your buttons. It's your choice, but somehow we both know that your button pushers do not have your happiness as their priority!

So what about *those* people? You know, the ones who push your buttons so relentlessly that sooner or later you think that you have to explode on them to make them go away. If you believe that blowing up will make them go away, then they will never really go away. It's like hitting the TV. You need to hit it more and more to get the same result, and finally you break it. Each time you choose to explode as a response to button pushers, you transfer your power and energy to them.

You empower *Them*. You have chosen to be out of control (OOC), and because of your actions, they are able to achieve their goal and your power. If this strategy works on you once, twice, three times, the button pusher begins to expect the transfer of power and knows that the strategy is effective. Children are masters of this technique, though if you are a parent or a button-pushing adult child, you know that already.

Everyone pushes emotional buttons. A current, like electricity, courses through our veins when the other person blows. Usually the jolt alone would be enough to make us feel as though we won, but the other person's acquiescence is the real proof of victory. Unfortunately, that's the bottom line. Winning by creating an emotionally unstable environment will result in winning a battle, but not the war. This kind of win is as unstable as the energy that went into attaining it. The results are never satisfying for very long, and there's a reason for that. Zev, in the following story, was able to achieve success for a short amount of time, but over the long run, his methods destabilized the workplace for everyone around him.

Pushing Buttons for Productivity

The administration thought that Zev was an efficient, effective manager. After six months on the job, productivity on his team was up and costs were down. Six months later, five of the eight people on Zev's team, workers who had been with the company for over five years, resigned. Searching for, hiring, and training the workers cost the company more than the profit they had made in the first year of Zev's employ. Turnover in Zev's department, even with new hires, was extremely high. Eventually the company had to reassign Zev to a different position.

Exit interviews with staff consistently referred to Zev's style of pitting team members against one another, creating an atmosphere of fear and anxiety of failure. False promises of grand success that never materialized were Zev's mantra. Zev learned how to push the buttons of the staff for quick results, but unfortunately, he lost the ability to keep them happy.

The behavioral tools in your toolbox have to be about getting to your goal. Your personal goal, however, does not exist in isolation. Getting to your goal will require that you interact with others and that you continue to live in the outside world. Your goal is tailored to you, but usually it's intricately tied to the goals of others, if only in keeping the emotional environments you enter stable.

Tool #1 takes this into account. Tools are usually problem-situation specific. Just as you would not use a broom to clean spilled olive oil or a wrench on your windshield, choose the tools to repair your emotional environment according to their effectiveness in the situation.

SITUATION

You find yourself in a highly charged, emotionally unstable environment.

Required tools: 1

Tool 1: Inner Drill for Goal Identification—a Stable Personal IE2

Goal identification is the first and most important tool for your toolbox. We all have long- and short-term goals, and since we don't live alone on this Earth, we need to constantly evaluate and reevaluate our goals to fit our needs and the needs of the world around us. As a change-partner, your first and primary goal will always be to keep the IE2 around you stable. Toss the hammer; it is totally ineffective for this goal. You will use the following bits in your inner drill:

- Honest, positive self-talk. Self-talk is exactly what it sounds like. You will need to engage in a conversation with yourself. Your mantra for this will be, "What do *I* want to have happen next?" To which you will answer, "I want to stabilize my IE2." Then you ask, "What can I do that will support my positive, stable IE2?" The final step is to look into your toolbox for the proper bit. Any of the following will probably work.
  o The seven Rs (chapter 7)
  o Breathing/relaxation exercises (chapter 16)
  o Know your Emotional Disaster Plan by heart, and share it with two people you trust. (chapter 10)
  o Choose to *act*. Do not react. (chapters 5,10)

SITUATION

No matter what you do, you find yourself engaged in relationship with people who never take into account your feelings or emotions. They are narrow-minded and live in a state of "emotional unconsciousness," where all the arrows point to themselves. These people cannot understand the importance of living with other people and their goals. They are concerned only with their own goals and happiness. They view others as being there to make sure that the person's goal is attained, regardless of the pain and instability this might bring into others' lives and environments.

Required tools: 1 and 2

Tool 2: Planned Decision-Making

In this situation, you would first use Tool 1 to determine how to get to a more stable IE2 before engaging in your active, planned decision-making. The diagram below, similar to the one in chapter three, walks you through how to make a true, planned decision. This tool, however, includes your positive and negative influences. Planned decisions require that you identify your goal, your immediate situation, your immediate intention, and a number (minimum of three) choices and probable outcomes.

GET TO YOUR
GOAL!

- **Goal.** The goal is only about *you*. What is your goal, regardless of the situation at hand? The goal needs to be concrete, observable, and measurable—a behavior, not a thought or state of being.
- **Present Situation.** What is the situation/event/person you are dealing with? Does it present a barrier to you reaching your goal, or will it help you get to your goal?
- **Intention.** This is an important aspect of your decision-making process. Will your action reflect an intention to get to the goal or react to the situation? As soon as the arrow of intention points to the situation instead of the goal, you have chosen reaction rather than action. Everything after this will then be directed toward the situation and will not help you achieve the goal.

- **Positive/Protective Factors.** These factors are people, support systems, and environments that help you sustain your forward momentum.
- **Negative/Risk Factors.** These factors are people, support systems, and environments that prevent you from moving toward your goals.
- **Choice/Likely Outcome.** This refers to a choice that you can make and the likely outcome from that choice.
- **Action.** This is the behavior you choose from your multiple alternatives.
- **Outcome.** This is the result you achieve from your chosen action.

Situation

You have just been given a task that you feel is well beyond your abilities; however, if you reject the task, you may lose the goal that you've been working for. Examples: You have been focused on moving into a management position, and you're given a job to work out a million-dollar budget for a project. Or, you've been writing a book for three years and you meet a publisher who's interested in seeing your manuscript. Or, you've been in a good relationship for a few months and the other person brings up the idea of making it permanent.

Required tools: 1, 2, 3, and 4

Tool 3: Self-Efficacy Using PRO Strategy

The bottom line is that you may not be ready for this task, and you might need to come to terms with that. If you're honest with yourself about your goal, however, this is the time to identify what skills are missing. In other words, what are the reasons you're afraid to say yes to the offer? When you identify these skills, break them down into their smallest parts and start to practice them. What is self-efficacy? Self-efficacy is capability that is based upon having a reliable skill. Very often self-efficacy is confused with self-esteem, which is feeling good about yourself. Self-esteem, however, can be easily deflated when the skill you pretend to have doesn't materialize when you need it. Self-efficacy, on the other hand, has a strong foundation you can rely on. It's based in ability and will allow you to demonstrate your capacity to get the job done. Using the PRO Strategy will help you develop the tool of self-efficacy. You will preemptively learn the skills that will become your foundation for accomplishing your goal. What you will be replacing in this situation is the lack of knowledge or skill to successfully complete the task.

Once you have the first skill down, practice it until it's a positive habitual response. Then start on the next needed task.

Tool 4: Strength Identification

What are your strengths? Frame who you are and what you want in a positive picture in your mind. Then create a list on paper or in your head. You may not have all the skills you need for this job, but you have certain strengths that will allow you to learn what you need to truly attain this goal. Humility is not a strength in this toolbox; humility is a strength when your ability is so strong and great that you no longer need to be your best marketing agent. If you're there already, you are probably a successful change-partner. State what you want to have happen in the positive, not the negative. Frame your goals by stating what you want, not what you want to avoid. Trash the statement, "I'm not the kind of person who .... "

SITUATION

Since you can remember, you can't identify one really happy moment that wasn't ruined for you. You always feel kind of anxious or sad—sometimes you describe yourself as "empty." You have a hard time getting excited or interested in anything that involves others, and you struggle sleeping through the night. When you heard about this book, you were heartened a little thinking that *maybe* it would help, but as you've been reading you've only felt less capable and hopeful.

Required tools: 5 and 4

Tool 5: Recognize the Need for Professional Help

Just as kicking the TV didn't repair it, beating yourself up for not meeting your own expectations, or feeling incapable of meeting the expectations of those around you and withdrawing from your friends and family, will not help you. This situation reflects symptoms of depression. Sometimes we, or people we love, need to seek professional help to achieve stable IE2s. Until you can get to a stable IE2, you are always at risk of losing sight of your goal or even being able to identify a personal goal. If you, or a loved one, is chronically depressed, it will be difficult to identify what you want to have happen next.

Too often depression is misinterpreted for laziness or another behavioral trait that is within our power to change. We don't expect people who are blind to see once we move them closer to the screen, or people with diabetes to get better because they use a sugar substitute. Likewise, we can't expect control from a person with depression, mania, or any other illness that affects the ability to engage in and complete activities of daily living. Metabolic diseases such as thyroid malfunction will affect a person's ability to control his or her moods.

Food allergies can also have behavioral effects. If you, or someone you live with, cannot find the energy to get help, then part of your emotional disaster plan should include seeking professional help. There is a saying that you are only as happy as the saddest person in your family. If that person needs a professional (doctor, nurse, therapist, nutritionist) to move to the capacity of establishing a stable IE2, then support that course of action.

TOOLBOX THIEVES

You can fill a toolbox to the brim; however, if you engage in behaviors that will undermine the efficacy of your tools, you might as well just keep your hammer at the ready. Toolbox thieves are as follows:

- o **WOUDACOULDASHOULDA Undermining alibis.** You only want to talk about getting to your goal. You already have all your excuses ready for your failure, and you've already made decisions that will prevent you from engaging in the behaviors you need to succeed.
- o **HUHWHAHUH? No personal goal/plan.** If you don't know where you are going, how can you know how to get there? Pretending that someone else's goals belong to you won't provide you with the sustained energy that you need to follow through.
- o **DONWANNAGROWUP? Nanny-nanny-poo-poo.** If you don't want to grow up, if you want to stay a baby all your life, then you're into the falling down part of walking, not the forward movement. Unfortunately, as you grow older, fewer and fewer people are going to want to clap at your baby steps between slips and falls. As time goes on, only enablers or sadists will want to stay around you.
- o **GOBBLESLURPBURP Eating and drinking habits.** Watch what you eat and drink. Foods and drinks will add or subtract to your ability to safely use your tools to maintain a stable IE2.
- o **WANNAHANGOUWIME? Friends and acquaintances.** Watch who you choose to hang around. Your choice in friends (fiends?) and acquaintances (accomplices?) will add or subtract

from your ability to access your tools and achieve/maintain/sustain your stable IE2.

Keeping your tools in top condition will make them more effective. Some conditioners that you can use to enhance your tools and organize your toolbox are called Boostfuls. Apply these Boostful products generously:

- **Care-ful.** Keep your eyes open to your changing environment.
- **Grate-ful.** Express thanks to the positive/protective people you invite into your life and to yourself for the positive work you do to achieve your IE2.
- **Purpose-ful.** Do things on purpose. Choose your changing environments, and choose your actions and admit to them.
- **Faith-ful.** When you are doing something that works, or you are with people who really help you, make sure you recognize what you are doing or who you are with and be sure to be faithful to them. Repeat the behaviors, and keep those people close.
- **Force-ful.** Do not overpower others in an attempt to establish a stable IE2. Allow your own force or energy to keep you stable, and then allow that stable force to support your happiness with yourself.
- **Happy-ful.** Hold on to your happiness. You are not responsible for the happiness of others. When you achieve a moment of happiness, stew in it, experience it, and smile about it. People who love you will be happy to see you so content.

SUMMARY

Strategies are useful tools to help you reach your goal. Too often we employ outdated or broken strategies that no longer support a forward momentum and that might actually keep us from achieving the goal. To fill our everyday lives with positive energy, creating an IE2 that keeps us smiling requires an awareness of ourselves, our needs, and our choice of actions.

CHAPTER 16

BEING HAPPY-FUL THROUGH HAPPINESS REGULATION

Anyone who has experienced a moment of pure joy, a sense of total well-being, knows what being happy-ful is all about. Happy-ful is different from happiness, joyousness, or elation. Happy-ful is a controllable, sustainable sense of well-being. Happy-ful is within your control. You might be asking, "If you have been able to connect with happiness, why regulate it? What's wrong with being ecstatically happy all the time?" It seems counterintuitive to most people that a feeling such as joy or happiness should be regulated. After all, hasn't this whole book been about learning how to identify, release, and celebrate the ability to stabilize your IE2 and experience happiness? Happiness, as opposed to happy-ful, is not stable. We experience happiness; we are capable of being happy-ful.

When you engage in extreme emotions, even if they are joyful, you could end up with a catastrophe, as Kam learned in the following story.

Extreme Emotion Is Highly Unstable

Teacher Z., had a practice of identifying the best student of the day. She would openly give that student praise and would then reward the student with a ten-minute early dismissal.

On this particular day, Kam, a student with learning disabilities and impulse control problems, was the student who was given the honor. He was greatly shocked by this, since he was usually the last to leave.

When Kam was given the privilege to be the first to leave, instead of packing his things and leaving, he gave into his sensation of extreme happiness and did a dance. Then he proceeded to insult some of the others in the class who regularly got recognition.

In response to his behavior, the teacher told him to sit back down. He stared at her in confusion. The teacher repeated the request in a tone of voice that was unmistakably an order. His response was to lift his chair into the air.

Kam was thinking, "If I lift the chair then it will be impossible for me to sit on it." Without thought to consequence, in his unstable IE2, he continued to hold the chair high, causing fear and panic in his classmates and teacher.

Kam had a limited toolbox and inexperience with extreme happiness in the school setting. His *reaction* had a terrible outcome. The teacher and students saw his behavior as threatening, and it resulted in Kam being suspended from school. When working with me on a short story, Kam decided that his story had a good moral: *It doesn't matter why you lose control of your response. Even happiness can lead to disaster if it isn't regulated.*

Kam didn't expect to get a reward from the teacher. The unexpectedness of the praise, rooted in the anticipation of the normal negative feedback, destabilized Kam's emotional environment.

MARSHALL'S LAW #12: Any extreme emotion can open the door to a disaster. Happiness, sadness, anger, and envy, when taken to the extreme, destabilize the emotional environment and create ideal conditions for an emotional tornado.

Giving in to any extreme emotion destabilizes your IE2. If left unchecked, it will destabilize the IE2s of those around you. We're all pretty good at identifying when a negative extreme emotion is brewing, and most of us can figure how to get out of the path of the oncoming, destructive tornado. It is more difficult, however, when the IE2 destabilization is due to a positive extreme emotion; we don't see the possible negative outcomes. This has been demonstrated again and again at football games, political elections, and any group celebration that promotes excessive alcohol consumption.

Being happy-ful is a skill that supports optimism. Optimism is an attitude that embodies hope. Confidence, buoyancy, and brightness are sometimes used as synonyms for optimism. A person who is optimistic is capable of seeing the positive side of an issue and is able to anticipate the happy ending. Optimism is the frame we can choose to place around an event or an experience to promote positive outcome thinking. Once you start practicing seeing the positive potential in a situation, you are able to start planning a route to getting to that destination.

Optimism and engaging in the practice of positive outcome decision-making skills can change your future. Optimism, it turns out, is not a trait or a genetic disposition; it's a learned skill.[15, 16] Conversely, helplessness and feelings of incapability are also learned. According to Martin Seligman, author of *Learned Optimism*, when we study the attributes of successful people we often overlook one component: the individual's optimistic attitude. Seligman asserts that despite having talent and a great desire for success, the ingredient that will either make or break a person's ability to sustain success will be the person's choice of optimism or pessimism. Despite popular belief, pessimism is not the opposite of optimism. Pessimists doubt the likelihood of a happy ending, but they don't discount it. A fatalist is the true antithesis of an optimist, because fatalists have no hope. Without hope, an optimist is a lost soul.

How can you learn to have hope and faith (be hope-ful and faith-ful) in the possibility of happy endings? After all, aren't we taught that happy endings only exist in fairy tales? Research teaches us that hope and belief in happy endings comes from our ability to make happy endings occur. The more successful you are at achieving small wins, the more likely you will achieve your goals and create your happy endings.

Optimism, Patience, and Persistence

RJ always believed that good things happened to the lucky. Unfortunately for RJ, luck never was the strong suit in his life. RJ's rich friends had big homes and fancy cars and took luxurious vacations. RJ always wanted to see the world. He wanted to have a management position with an international firm that would support his love of travel, but he didn't know anyone in the business. RJ decided to work for a hotel chain for three years, investing five hundred dollars a month with a trusted accountant into a high-yield account.

RJ lived frugally and was so enchanted with his experiences that "life is wonderful" became his daily mantra. Over the course of three years, RJ traveled to many lands, learned multiple languages, and met a partner with whom every day was better than the last. Upon returning to the United States, RJ learned that his investments had tripled and the hotel chain had opened an office in the states and needed a manager. RJ applied for and was hired into the new management position. After about a year, a new employee came up to RJ and said, "You are so lucky; you have a dream job. I'm never lucky."

RJ smiled and replied, "It's not about luck; it's about knowing what you want and not being in too much of a rush to get there."

Learning how to be optimistic will have an impact on your decision-making and your health. It is a demonstrated fact that optimists are in better physical health and are more socially successful than pessimists.[17, 18] Is it any wonder that they're happy? A fatalist would say that being happy-ful is impossible. I say let the fatalist talk to Mohammed Ali, who once made this comment:

"Impossible is not a fact. It's an opinion. Impossible is not a declaration. It's a dare. Impossible is potential. Impossible is temporary."

He should know; he achieved the impossible time and again!

Since 1988 I have been practicing what I call "orthodox optimism." This is not a religion, though to get the full benefit of the program one must carry out the rituals religiously every day. In orthodox optimism, the process is key. Enjoying the preparation and the journey to the goal provides the emotional soil that fertilizes and nourishes an optimistic outlook. After all, if your goal is to own your own home, then the road to attaining it is planning a future that will assure you an income that can meet your mortgage payments. Choosing a job that brings you joy, working with others who are like you, and taking the time to do your job right makes each day rewarding, while also leading you to your ultimate goal. Optimism is built through the action of identifying what makes you happy, planning how to engage in that activity each day, and enjoying yourself while you do it.

There are rituals we can choose to engage in that lead to a happy-ful life, and there are ways to open yourself to the optimistic frame. Once you take the rituals to heart and they become positive habits in your daily experience, you can add them to your toolbox. Make these rituals a part of your daily experience. You must actively, mindfully, thoughtfully, and consciously engage in doing each of these actions every day.

- **Concentrate 100 percent on the task at hand.** Stop multitasking. If you are on the phone, concentrate on the conversation; if you are eating dinner with friends, enjoy their company. Turn off the Blackberry, the cell phone, and the beeper. Give 100 percent of yourself to what you are doing. Finish one task before launching into another. If what you are doing is not satisfying, determine how to cut it short and make a mental note not to do it again.

- **Smile as often and hard as you can.** It doesn't matter if you're happy. Empty your brain and start smiling. Once you start smiling, you actually trigger your brain into releasing hormones that will facilitate good thoughts. Feel your smile. Feel your whole body as you smile. Smile hard—till it hurts—from ear to ear! Don't worry, nothing bad will happen. It's the first step to being happy-ful. It's amazing that when you walk around smiling, people smile back!

- **State the "just what I wanted" mantra.** What ever happens to you in your day, realize that it happened because of choices you made up to that moment. So, whatever happens it must be because it was "just what you wanted" to have happen. Miss the bus to work? Say out loud, "Oh, this was just what I wanted to have happen. I stayed up late last night, woke up late this morning, missed having coffee, and ran all the way to the bus stop because I really wanted to miss the bus! If I had wanted to make the bus, I would have gone to bed earlier, woken up earlier, and made sure I was here on time." People around you might stare, but after you get the hang of it, it will usually get you to smile. Moreover, it should actually help you make "just what I wanted to happen" events more positive.

- **Express gratitude to the people who have made, and continue to make, your life better.** Be aware of the small and large things that people do on a daily basis that help you have a good life. Make a list of what you feel you do that others should be grateful for. If you have a partner, exchange your personal lists and begin to thank each other.

- **Stop complaining!** No matter what, simply take responsibility for how things are and figure out what you want to have happen next. Don't rely on someone else to rescue you or "make you happy." They won't, and complaining will only make you miserable and miserable to be around.

- **Focus on the good!** Refuse to engage in gossip, no matter what. Feel certain that anything you say *will* be repeated, and you *will be* held accountable for it. Only say about others what you would like to have come back to you twofold. If you don't like someone, don't spend any of your brainpower thinking about him or her. This negative, time-wasting behavior is a classic happy-ful life leak!

- **Breathe!** It's surprising how many people can't do this. Take time every day to just listen to your own breathing. In with the good air through the nose, out with the old, stale air through the mouth. If you have plants, do it around them; they'll appreciate the carbon dioxide you're providing. Put a nonsense word into your brain while you breath to stop yourself from multitasking. I like "drack nee cah poh." "Drak nee" for inhaling and "cah poh" for exhaling.

- **Open up to new thoughts.** Actively listen to what people are saying to you, and mindfully consider their approach to the situation. Consider how different your life would be if you were born onto this Earth as them. Look at the same situation from multiple perspectives. Before disagreeing or dismissing what someone is saying to you, say, "I've never thought of it like that before." Then smile.

- **Move your body.** Engage in at least thirty minutes of exercise every day. Dance, walk, take the stairs instead of the elevator, ride a bike, or go for a swim. Get your heart pumping, and don't forget to smile while you're doing it!

You can achieve a happy-ful life by engaging in the orthodox optimist rituals and living by your word. Identify who you want to be, describe your positive traits (both the ones you have and the ones you want to have), and then actively engage in, or model, that behavior.

Of course there are rituals we engage in that are not optimistic, nor are they positive. Sometimes our habitual behaviors and the behaviors of our significant others don't always lead us to the outcomes we were hoping for.

Moving Past Habitual Family Stereotypes

CC was the baby in the family, and despite the fact that fifty years had passed since CC's birth, the family still insisted on identifying the traits that CC exhibited in the first decade as the cornerstone of her personality. Usually when they all got together, a disagreement would occur and the happy get-together would quickly disintegrate into an insult contest.

"I'm the smart one," CC's sister said one holiday gathering. "JJ is the lucky one, BB is the talented one, and CC you're ... well, you're the spoiled baby—the pouting distraction!" The family laughed and stared at CC to see what kind of outburst this insult would initiate.

CC smiled at her family and replied, "That's an interesting, though somewhat sad and narrow take on our family relations. Personally, I've never seen us like that." Then turning to her mother added, "Great dinner. Do you want help clearing the table?"

"A wonderful offer—thank you," replied CC's mother.

CC smiled, picked up a plate, and left the room.

CC's choice of acting rather than reacting modeled a behavior that reflected who CC is, not the person described by the sister. Family gatherings can be the most volatile environments. They put us in situations that stir up old, habitual behaviors, many of which are painful and negative. At the same time, family gatherings have the potential to be the most rewarding, as long as we realize how to behave in them.

Happy-ful lives are good in all environments. A rabbi once told me, "Family is God's way of teaching us how to get along with people we don't always like." I laughed when I heard it and then repeated it a few times, understanding the truth that it spoke. Family is family, and like them or not, we have them for life. We don't choose our first families, the ones we are born or adopted into. We don't choose the children we rear; they come to us as individual packages with specific likes, dislikes, and personalities. Learning to live with them in harmony, peace, and even love sets the stage for a happy-ful existence.

Sometimes the reality of family conflicts with the "perfect family," "perfect child," and "perfect life" we fantasize about. This behavior unconsciously sets us at battle with the family, child, and life we have, fostering dissatisfaction rather then acceptance of what is. Once we can accept what is, we can identify how to achieve a personal level of happiness.

A mindful change-partner understands that *now*, the present moment, is the best time for making positive memories. Today is tomorrow's yesterday. Memories are made up of things and emotions that we choose to concentrate on in the present. Each one of us has the choice to create our own positive memories by focusing on the best part of each day. For a change-partner, the goal of the game of life is to ride the wave of the happy-ful life, enjoying every moment. Change-partners get into ruts, but they also know how to get out of them. A happy-ful life doesn't occur without practice; it takes daily work developing and perfecting our planned action skills to stay on track.

Self-determination, being responsible for your actions, yields high results. Choosing to chase the tornado, watch the lightning on a golf course, or skydive without a parachute might be exciting to some, but it can get old very fast! Slowly replacing negative, habitual behaviors and thoughts with positive ones will put you in tune with a deeper level of excitement—happy-ful excitement that lasts and permeates all aspects of your life. Self-determined or regulated emotional behavior will impact your personal IE2, as well as the IE2s of those around you. Moreover, it will draw new positive people into your circle.

As you grow into a more positive person, you may notice that some old friends who are negative people will no longer be comfortable around you. They might even eliminate themselves from your social circle. Happy-ful lives are constructed by learning how to enjoy the journey as well as the destination. Finding joy in the process of getting to your goals supports your sense of contentment with the present and feeds your positive memory bank.

Summary

Developing a belief in yourself and an understanding that you alone are responsible for your future is not a secret. It's not a magical potion that you drink or a spell someone casts on you. It is a way of life—a commitment to yourself needed to own the achievement of a working, happy-ful life. It is the skill of opening your mind to the possibility that where some people see the ending, you are willing to discover the opportunity that can lead you to becoming who you always wanted to be—with a never-ending new and better beginning every day.

CHAPTER 17

THE BEGINNING

Welcome to the beginning of the rest of your life. It's up to you, and always has been, to decide whether to choose to be happy or to renew your membership in the BMC Club.

Before showing you the door to the rest of your life, I want to turn your attention to the word *change*. This whole book, and your life, is about change. It's about growing up and growing older. It's about keeping what works and tossing out what doesn't. It's about becoming aware of your potential, your risks, and your emotional environments. It's about factoring all this in and engaging in a plan of action that you have carefully chosen after anticipating the outcomes and weighing the options.

It's not about changing jobs, relationships, or countries of residence. Happy-ful lives are rich and *stable*. Mindful change-partners are committed to accepting and acting upon the changes inherent in life and cultivating the support systems that fill a life with joy and meaning. Active change-partners are not addicted to the thrill of the change for the sake of the change. They are, on the other hand, thrilled at the opportunity to accept the challenge presented by the change. The more successful we are in working with change, the more desirable our lives look to those on the outside. Chasing change for change's sake is a description of escapism, not of a change-partner In fact, being a successful change-partner actually can present you with a mousetrap that has been known to topple the best of us.

THE LURE OF LIVING A HAPPY-FUL LIFE

The ultimate change-partner mousetrap: beware! People who are inherently dissatisfied with their lives will think your life is magical. After all, you will be happy, satisfied, and successful. Of course these outcomes are a result of you working to become who you could have been, every day. They are the payoff of paying attention to the details of the life you want and having the capacity of making your dreams reality. Does this mean that the change-partner doesn't have an Achilles' heel—a point of weakness that when stroked fills the change-partner with self-doubt and tempts us away from the very behaviors that have given us our happy-ful lives? Beware the individual who destabilizes your IE2 at a time when you love your life!

The change that invigorates a change-partner to becoming who he or she could have been is the capability of choosing action rather than reaction, of consciously monitoring and expressing gratitude to the people who make life better. Personal change is embraced within the context of a goal, not as a response to temptation. If there is an environment or a habit that the change-partner is addicted to, it is maintaining emotional stability. Change that reflects reaction rather than action usually destabilizes the IE2, which is the opposite outcome a change-partner seeks. As you begin your journey to becoming who you could have been, remember that small changes lead to small successes. Over time, small successes establish a foundation of self-efficacy and a reality-based hope of happy endings.

Huge behavior changes and swings between emotional extremes create vacuums. Vacuums are highly unstable and need to be filled. Behavior and emotional vacuums will suck in whatever is closest, not necessarily what will lead you to the goal you want. When you achieve your happiness, it might be a lure for those who want a quick fix to happiness. Beware of the happy-ful wannabes!

The Lure of The Happy-ful Wannabe

On KZ's sixtieth birthday, JP, a very attractive, young individual, approached and began to plant seeds of desire—desire for more money, more power, more youth, and more freedom. KZ was tempted to respond with reckless abandon and follow the trail to the "better" life with JP until a friend stepped in.

"Why do you think JP is so insanely attracted to you? It's because of what you have accomplished, your achievements and your success in attaining happiness with your family and your business. What is it that JP offers to your life—a chance to change it all?"

"Yes, that and youth, a new beginning, freedom," KZ answered as if in a daze.

"And you think another human being can give you that?" the friend mused. "JP thinks that if you can be made to be unsatisfied with your life, you will leave us all. How will that make you happy? JP wants the life you have now, but if you walk away from it you won't have that to offer anymore ... and you won't have us either. This life you have now is successful because of the choices you've made up to now with us, your friends and family members who have supported you. Turn your back on your support, and you'll be starting a new life all right, but not necessarily a good beginning. Living in hotels is fun at first, but there's nothing like coming home."

KZ looked from his good friend to the lure of youth and vitality. "It sure is tempting," KZ said.

"So is skateboarding, but let's leave it to them who don't have as much to lose!"

"Besides" added KZ, "I hate hotels". The two friends laughed and turned from JP.

When your skills are sharpened, and your successes begin to mount, do not take them for granted. You are only as good as your ability to utilize the tools in your toolbox today.

When you are not determining what your goal is, or you think that you can make anyone else besides yourself happy, you will start down a slippery slope to the land of undermining alibis and BMCers. The good news is that once you realize where you are headed, an experienced change-partner can stop, breathe, implement the seven Rs, and set a new course toward the goal of reestablishing a stable IE2 to work from.

Once you've lived in the happy-ful zone, it's painful to leave but usually fairly easy to negotiate your way back. All it requires is honesty, acceptance of the need to change your attitude, and focused concentration on the goal you want to achieve.

SUMMARY

There's no secret to creating a happy-ful life. It's not written backwards in a numerological code that can only be deciphered on a full moon by true believers. It is choosing to engage in the purposeful next fifteen minutes of your life. Becoming who you always wanted to be—Becoming You—is about developing and practicing the skills that allow you to plan and execute actions that move you to your goal—every day.

You know, the stuff that change-partners thrive on!

So, what do *you* want to have happen next? Are you ready to continue on the journey of becoming *you*? Okay, then put the book down and get to it!

MARSHALL'S LAWS

MARSHALL'S LAW #1: Lack of time is not a valid excuse.

MARSHALL'S LAW #2: Your behavior cannot depend on someone else. You are in control of yourself, your choices, and your behavior. **Using other people as an excuse for not succeeding is no longer valid (and will, over time, turn into an undermining alibi).**

MARSHALL'S LAW #3: You are responsible for everything that is in your life; you can choose to make snap decisions, habitual decisions, or planned decisions. You know that choosing snap or habitual decisions reduces your control over future circumstances or outcomes, but it is your choice to make those decisions over planned choices. **Using fate, luck, or the impact of other people's choice on your life are no longer valid excuses.**

MARSHALL'S LAW #4: Despite popular belief, **wishing and hoping are not courses of action!**

MARSHALL'S LAW #5: You are responsible for the life you have right now. **Every choice you have made, up to an including today, has created the life you lead at this moment.**

MARSHALL'S LAW #6: You are *only* **in control of your response to your environment.** When you choose to give up control of your behavioral response, either through snap or habitual decision-making, you have chosen to relinquish your control over your future. Someone else *will* step in, and your behavior has given the permission.

MARSHALL'S LAW #7: Emotional tornadoes are never worth the thrill of the ride! Preparation in advance is the only antidote. Once you're on the ride, you have chosen reaction over action. Your control over your ability to act is gone. *Get to safety before making any major decisions!*

MARSHALL'S LAW #8: Accepting things because "that's the way things are" produces a false sense of comfort. **To become accustomed to and to support behaviors because they occur in a predictable, repeating pattern is a recipe for disaster.**

MARSHALL'S LAW #9: You cannot expect anyone else to save you. Hoping and wishing are not action verbs, nor are they reliable plans of action to get out of the vacuum of loss. Each person must develop skills to save him or herself. **Waiting to be rescued will no longer be accepted as a valid strategic plan of action.**

MARSHALL'S LAW #10: All change is loss. Plan for it, and understand that loss of any kind will produce a vacuum. All vacuums are unstable and seek to be stabilized. Before you change a behavior, learn your replacement behavior.

MARSHALL'S LAW #11: It is the craftsperson, not the tool, that brings success. The tools in your toolbox are only as effective as the person who uses them. A tool used incorrectly or on the wrong job will not successfully achieve the desired goal. The more practice the user has, the better the tool performs.

MARSHALL'S LAW #12: Any extreme emotion can open the door to a disaster. Happiness, sadness, anger, and envy, when taken to the extreme, destabilize the emotional environment and create ideal conditions for an emotional tornado.

FOOTNOTES

1. M. Csíkszentmihályi, *Beyond Boredom and Anxiety* (San Francisco: Jossey-Bass, 1975).

2. Z. Klein, "The Ethological Approach to the Study of Human Behavior," *Neuroendocrinology,* Letters 21, no.6 (2000): 447–481.

3. National Severe Storms Laboratory. Severe Thunderstorm Climatology. 8/29/2003. http://www.nssl.noaa.gov/hazard/ (accessed 6/09/2005).

4. C. Peterson, S. F. Maier, and M. E. P. Seligman,. *Learned Helplessness: A Theory for the Age of Personal Control* (New York: Oxford University Press, 1995).

5. H. Ginott, *Between Parent & Child: New Solutions to Old Problems* (New York: Macmillan, 1965).

6. B. Rothchild, *The Body Remembers the Psychophysiology of Trauma and Trauma Treatment* (New York: W.W. Norton, 2000).

7. D. Goleman, *Emotional Intelligence* (New York: Bantam, 1995).

8. D. Goleman. *Vital Lies, Simple Truths* (New York: Simon and Schuster, 1985) p.95.

9. D. Goleman. *Vital Lies, Simple Truths.* (New York: Simon and Schuster, 1985) p. 96.

10. D. Goleman. *Vital Lies, Simple Truths.* (New York: Simon and Schuster, 1985).

11. E. Kubler-Ross, *On Grief and Grieving: Finding the Meaning of Grief Through the Five Stages of Loss* (New York: Simon and Schuster, 2005).

12. F. Heider, *The Psychology of Interpersonal Relationships* (New York: John Wiley & Sons, 1958).

13. C. Peterson, G. M. Buchanan, & M. E. P. Seligman, *Explanatory Style: History and Evolution of the Field,* eds. G. M. Buchanan and M. E. P. Seligman (Hillsdale, NJ: Lawrence Erlbaum, 1995) 1–20.

14. I. Ajzen, "Perceived Behavioral Control, Self-Efficacy, Locus of Control and Theory of Planned Behavior," *Journal of Applied Social Psychology vol.* 32 no.4 (2006): 665–683.

15. D. Mithaug, *Self-Determined Kids: Raising Satisfied and Successful Children* (Lexington, MA: Lexington Books, 1991).

16. M. Seligman, *Learned Optimism: How to Change Your Mind and Your Life* (New York: Alfred A. Knopf, 1998).

17. K. Karren, K., B. Hafen, N. L. Smith, and K. Frandsen. *Mind/Body/Health: The Effects of Attitudes, Emotions and Relationships* (San Francisco: Benjamin Cummings, 2003).

18. M. Seligman, *Learned Optimism: How to Change Your Mind and Your Life* (New York: Alfred A. Knopf, 1998).

Printed in the United States
217018BV00001B/1/P